2013

EVIDENCE OF THINGS NOT SEEN

Ann —

With great Joy, I give you the Blessed and anointed book of God to minister to you! It has been a pleasure knowing you and watching you blossom in Faith —

Love Always in Him
Barbara

A BOOK OF POEMS

BARBARA KELLY

EVIDENCE OF THINGS NOT SEEN

TATE PUBLISHING
AND ENTERPRISES, LLC

Published by Tate Publishing & Enterprises, LLC
127 E. Trade Center Terrace | Mustang, Oklahoma 73064 USA
1.888.361.9473 | www.tatepublishing.com

Tate Publishing is committed to excellence in the publishing industry. The company reflects the philosophy established by the founders, based on Psalm 68:11,
"The Lord gave the word and great was the company of those who published it."

Book design copyright © 2013 by Tate Publishing, LLC. All rights reserved.
Cover design by Rtor Maghuyop
Interior design by Jake Muelle

Published in the United States of America

ISBN: 978-1-62295-843-6
Poetry / Subjects & Themes / Inspirational & Religious
13.02.08

FOREWORD

It has been said… "One Word From God Can Change Your Life Forever"… In this book you will find many such words. I have known both the Author of this book and the secretary who took His dictation for many years. Barbara Kelly espouses no authorship or ownership over the words contained in this book only a stewardship responsibility for which she feels deeply humbled. She attributes their origin to the LORD. I have no doubt that this is true; both because of my knowledge of her, and also because of my personal relationship with many of the words which you will read in this book.

I happen to have the unique distinction of being the first person Barbara was ever directed to give one of these words to personally. It is universally acknowledged that each word contained in this book is for everyone and anyone as the Spirit of the LORD wills, reveals, and directs, in His due season. But my testimony as the recipient of the first of these words to be delivered to an individual is that she gave it to me at a time when God had spoken to me of great change and transition coming to my life of which she was not aware.

For many months I had been collecting 'little stones' (as Hannah Hurnard would say in Hinds Feet on High Places) of revelation, rhema, and promise. Collecting them as the LORD willed in times of private prayer and pain, communion and questioning, and meditation upon His Holy Word (Bible), I had hidden them in my heart and no one but the LORD and I knew. That is until the day that the enemy of our soul tried to tip the scales in his favor and the LORD knew I desperately needed a word of comfort and confirmation regarding all that He had been telling me and showing me along this journey on which I undeniably found myself. It was then that I heard the phone ring (at a time when I normally would not have answered a phone call) and looked down through my tears and saw Barbara's name on the caller ID. Out of respect for the anointing I knew to be on her life, I took the call and heard these words:

> EXTREME MEASURES HAVE BEEN TAKEN TO SEPARATE THE WHEAT FROM THE CHAFF
> THE OIL HAS BEEN POURED
> SWEET WINE ACCOMPANIES
> THE CHOSEN REMNANT REMAINS

Over the course of the next four years these words, much like the scriptures, would reveal different aspects of themselves to me each time I would pray and meditate over them. But always, I would know that no matter what changes and transitions were in store for me, the LORD had already prepared the oil and the wine, the anointing and the grace that it would take to successfully transition from each extreme measure and separation that He had ordained for me along the way.

As you hold this book in your hands, I bless you as its reader, praying that its words will empower you to prosper in whatever season of your journey you may find yourself. My prayer of blessing is taken from I Thessalonians 5: 15-23 and 28: Amplified

See that none of you repays another with evil for evil, but always aim to show kindness and seek to do good to one another and to everybody.

Be happy (in your faith) and rejoice and be glad-hearted continually (always).

Be unceasing in your prayer (praying perseveringly);

Thank (God) in everything (no matter what the circumstances may be, be thankful and give thanks), for this is the will of God for you (who are) in Christ Jesus (the Revealer and Mediator of that will).

Do not quench (suppress or subdue) the (Holy) Spirit;

Do not spurn the gifts and utterances of the prophets (do not depreciate prophetic revelations nor despise inspired instruction or exhortation or warning).

But test and prove all things (until you can recognize) what is good; (to that) hold fast.

Abstain from evil (shrink from it and keep aloof from it) in whatever form or whatever kind it may be.

And may the God of peace Himself sanctify you through and through (separate you from profane things, make you pure and wholly consecrated to God); and may your spirit and soul and body be preserved sound and complete (and found) blameless at the coming of our LORD Jesus Christ (the Messiah).

The grace (the unmerited favor and blessings) of our LORD Jesus Christ (the Messiah) be with you all. Amen, (so be it).

In His Name,
Denise Harrison Garlick

1

❧

My tender heart
Is needy
Your blessed assurance
To this daughter of
Zion
Redeems me
From
Myself

❧

Oh, Savior
How do I express
My gratitude
Where to begin

❧

I beseech
You, loving Father
Open up in me
What has been
Closed

❧

Restore the gifts
I plead
Prepare my spirit
My heart and
Mind
To receive the
Magnitude of
What You have in
Store

❧

I receive
I believe

❧

It's time to say
What no man
Could imagine

❧

Light of my life
Illuminate

❧

Angels congregate
Let all the
Earth
Rejoice

2

❧

It is written in the wind
The destiny
The many hues of creation
Suggest a force
Beyond vision
Forge in me Your plan
Awaken my immortal soul
To the untold, fathomless
Depths of You

❧

Creator, come
Create in me
Your destiny

❧

I have seen the
Place
I have seen the
Wealth
Remarkable

3

❧

The path I've taken
Is not easy
The world interferes
In my intense desire
To walk—not stumble
With You

❧

A space in time
My mind does rhyme
Set to the music of You

❧

The path is littered with
My unimaginable history.
Stepping stones or stumbling
Blocks—my choice

❧

My dear, wonderful Friend
Knowing You has its
Merits
Peace
Joy
Mercy
Eternal grace
Keep me on the road
Less traveled
On stepping stones

❧

❦

Grasping Truth
Hearing confusion
Seeing a vision
Speaking from the Spirit
What joy
To know You prevail
Oh, Holy One of Israel

❦

How can I believe
What I cannot see
How can I see
What I cannot believe

❦

A manufactured peace
Must be maintained
The only Peace to manifest
Its Truth comes from
Within and is protected
By the relationship from
Which it comes.

❦

Let Truth awaken
Confusion depart
The vision manifest
Spirit speaking never cease

❦

❦

Hiccups are a mystery
Puppy dogs epitomize cute
I awaken to a New Song
And know the Truth

❦

Listen to the wind
It is blowing
And whispering
Watch all creation
It speaks of You
Turn over a rock
And hear the hallelujah

❦

What will the wind say,
Creation speak
Rocks cry out
When You return
Riding on a cloud

❦

Bless the LORD, oh my soul

❦

6

When the morning is over
I'll take the joy
Move into a day of
extraordinary
Blessing
Knowing when night returns
Joy will come in the morning

When I reflect
Sometimes the good
Outweighs the bad
Sometimes I see
More bad
Let my reflections
Reveal
The truth in You
With boundless Mercy

Friendships are fragile
A trembling feather
In the wind
Relationships built
Upon the Rock
Cannot bend so far
They break

7

Swinging back and forth
The sky looks close
When I'm at the top
The earth too close
When I come down
Lead me to the Rock
That is so much
Higher than me

Lingering in the hope
That promises a
Future
Leaves no room
For the mind to fracture or
The emotions to
Betray
The promises are true
Hope is real
When flowing from
The throne of God

Barbara Kelly

8

∽

Be still
And know
That I am God
In the stillness
I hear Your voice
Leave me never,
Cries my soul
I know that You
Are God

∽

How do I know
You ask
My spirit reveals
His voice; my very
Being stands in awe
Of Him

∽

When pigs fly
When geese walk
When men bray
And donkeys talk
I'll still know who You are

∽

9

∽

No more need to facilitate
Or
Take in all I see
My time is consumed
By the Consuming Fire
Of the eternal plan
I see in You

∽

Perhaps there is no merit
In writing these things
Down
Again there is merit
In all You say

∽

I hear You say
I love you, child
It's such a
Beautiful revelation
Of my importance
To The One who
Created me

∽

10

❦

Do You remember me
Do I register in
Your registry
Where am I
That You are not
In noisy confusion
Or solitude
I'm surrounded
By You

❦

Not a note in
Rhyme of song
Not a paragraph
In prose
Not a newfound
Talent
Or repertoire
Just me hearing You
Doesn't a voice in
My head resemble You

❦

11

❦

I carry a resemblance
To those who say
I look more like
My Father
Than my family

❦

A switch was made
At birth
I became royalty

❦

A lover steeped in sorrow
For all lost loves
Will wander through
A door opened
To find
The Lover of her soul

❦

Opportunity seems shaky
But that could be just me
I let go while You hang on
To the investment made
In Heaven and
Throughout eternity

❦

Barbara Kelly

12

Could I know
Had I listened
How to see
If I were not
Blind
Come, Holy Spirit
Resurrect
My mind
Open my eyes to see
And my ears to hear

Sometimes my drum
Is not beating
Different or
Otherwise
So I listen for the
Distant call
To draw
And seal me
Under
Powerful wings

13

A flickering flame
Mesmerizing
A blazing fire
Kills
The winter of my
Soul
Is warmed
By that other
Fire
Smoldering to
Keep winter away

Shall I tell you of the ways
He has moved me
From precept to precept
From lower
To higher
From this realm
Into the next
Watching
As I go
The ramifications
Of the wicked

14

❧

Can I say
Hello
To the dreamer
No shame
Welcome
All who dream
Creator
Complete

❧

Somewhere deeper
Take me
Somewhere higher
Fly me
Move me
From this place
Translate me
It's a beautiful thing
To walk instead
Of run
To know Your Peace
While covered
In Divine Love

❧

15

❧

Somewhere
Sometime
Someplace
I will find
My destiny

❧

Completed

❧

Where to look
How to see
Only You
None
Of me
Intricately woven
Are the threads
Of my life
A golden path
Forever straight
From Heaven on
Through to return
One day to my
God

❧

Barbara Kelly

16

꩜

It's a heady thing
A waltz in rhythm
A beautiful flow
Between You
And me

꩜

Come into this
Place
Where mind
Must subside and
Spirit arise
To the occasion
Of Love

꩜

No more night
I perceive a new
Beginning
Nothing will remain
Of the old
We are renewed
To soar

꩜

17

꩜

Hues of blue
Saw my eyes
Of sorrow
Hues of blinding
Brilliance
In my view
Of You

꩜

Complete abandon
Wrapped in You
Where do I
Begin
To tell why
I know there is
No end
To this bliss

꩜

Spring, summer
Fall, and winter
Blend together in
The many hues
Of You

꩜

18

❧

Wide-eyed wonder
Towering success
Illuminating the cells
Of my being

❧

Forever a grateful
For Your
True and rich
Reward just for
Knowing You

❧

Sweet Spirit
Compel me
To be all
You planned
For me

❧

Holy, holy, holy
Is the Lamb
That was slain
Before the foundations
Of the world

❧

19

❧

Light of my life
Shine bright
I need You
Arrange my thoughts
To look like Yours

❧

Move in
Go with me
Wherever I go
Come, Holy Spirit
I'm anticipating
An overhaul
On my
Disposition
Sweeter as I go
Lighter, free
Bubbly

❧

Winsome Entity
Sing and dance
Over me

❧

20

It's a witty idea
I'm searching
A fandangled
Plan
With purpose
A beginning and
An end
Somewhere in the
Middle
I know
For sure
It's the grandeur
Of You

21

A sudden thing
Awakened me
To my worst
Reality

A stubborn resolve
From deep within
Says
I'm offended
By deafness
In others'
Ears

Why can't I realize
That no one really
Cares
But You

22

❧

I've questioned You
Are You really near
Do You really care
Why am I
Not healed
Not prospered
Why is my hand
Slackened
To do only what I
Want to do

❧

Severe coldness of heart
Threatens
A need to close off
In order not to offend

❧

In the midst of this
Oppression
I know
I'm persuaded
You are the One True God
My Father

❧

23

❧

Help
So another day is here
Help
So I resolve to cast
These emotions on You
To do only what
I know to do

❧

Simply open
My eyes
To see Truth
As You see

❧

Cure my blindness

❧

Do You hear me

❧

24

❧

He says he loves me
How can that be
When he doesn't know
Me
He says he wants me
How can that be
When he doesn't know
Me
If I were plain
Unadorned
Simple
Humble in all my ways
Would he really
Crave me

❧

I'm so confused
What do You want

❧

No mere lies
Make it real

❧

25

❧

There's a sanctuary
Between reality
And fiction
One keeps me grounded
The other feeds
Creativity

❧

I'll linger in smoldering
Flames of the expanded mind
Fuelled by an expansive
Spirit

❧

Soar, my beautiful spirit
Take me
Where I cannot see
Where clouds no longer
Darken

❧

26

⊷

Have I ever wished
Upon a star or
Seen a wish
Come true

⊷

Have I ever prayed,
Believed, witnessed
Heaven's answer

⊷

I am a dreamer of
Dreams
Not accomplished
By earthly means

⊷

Moved not by all
I see
Only by Thee

⊷

27

⊷

Sweaters, rings
Soft things
Surround me

⊷

Mighty God
Sweep over my
Spirit with
Fire and new
Beginnings

⊷

Awaken the center of
My being
Arise, Holy Spirit
Speak

⊷

I sit in my soft
Surroundings
Waiting for a
Mighty Fire to
Consume me

⊷

Barbara Kelly

28

❧

Quarrelling with You
Is very satisfying
Never judged
Always loved
Restored and blessed

❧

Sweet fragrance of You
Satisfy
I'm totally taken
By Your beauty

❧

The undertaker
Came
I escaped
Into You

❧

29

❧

Hope deferred
Makes a heart
Sick
Life steeped in
Hope from You
Awakens me
From slumber
Compels me
To tingling
Anticipation

❧

Whoa doggies
Moving forward
With arms stretched
Into timelessness
How to slow
When there's a
Need to run

❧

30

᪣

Sometimes
I resolve
To behave
As You would

᪣

Sometimes
I behave as
I would

᪣

Sometimes I would
As You would

᪣

This is ultimate
No greater cause

᪣

31

᪣

Not a mandate
A request
To live as though
Tomorrow
Would not come

᪣

Hey there
Outside my peripheral
What do You need
From me
How do I
Respond
Selflessly
Is what He asks

᪣

He will take care of me

᪣

Barbara Kelly

32

❧

This time
Not from inside
My head

❧

This time
Spirit led

❧

This time
When all men
Would interfere
None can

❧

This time
I'm rested
Grounded
Supernaturally
Hounded

❧

33

❧

Creatures of habit
Restless
Wrestling and
Challenged
By conformity
Hopelessly bound

❧

Set free by
Unfettered You
To live

❧

What is my heart
Saying
Where is the
Spirit teaching
By the speed
Of light
I walk
Into the place
I'm called

❧

34

❧

Make me invisible
Seen only by You
Bound in Your
Embrace
Under Your wings
Let these words
Bring You glory

❧

I allow only
The presence of You
To inhabit

❧

Somewhere there is
More
Show me

❧

You tower

❧

35

❧

I became holy
Inside Your
Grace
No other way
Erase the
Essence of me
To become
You in the
Earth
Go figure

❧

Can I vault
Over this
Chasm and
Be transformed
You say yes
Wow

❧

Barbara Kelly

36

❧

Faith in You
Is all I need
Your word
Is true
I have faith
In You

❧

You honor
Yourself and
Cannot lie
You honor
Your Word and
Watch over it
To perform it

❧

My wish
Freely hearing You
Discerning Your word

❧

37

❧

No obstacles
Do I receive
No doors are shut
All are now
Open for
Receiving
The open window
Pouring
Into my being

❧

Let understanding
Come
I'm receiving
Loving
Listening

❧

I will walk
Run
Toward the higher
Calling

❧

38

❧

I worship
The Author and
Finisher of my
Faith
I worship the
Jew
Who died to
Save this gentile
I worship the
Father whose
Spirit I harbor

❧

No more a secret
How much I
Love the
Wonderful God
The Captain
Of my salvation

❧

39

❧

Somewhere between
Where I was and
Where I am
The years
Reveal
A truth
A covenant
Not to be broken
By me or Him
On we go
I know I'll
See more as
I yield,
Ask
Receive
I receive

❧

40

✖

There is fertile ground
Pour water in
See the harvest
Ripe—ready
I am made
Rich and
You add no
Sorrow
Hallelujah

✖

Come forth, I
Call
From the dark
Places of earth
Where rust plunders
Cry no more for
Your
Rightful owner
Come
Even now
Come

✖

41

✖

You live in the flame
The sun, moon, and
Stars—You are in
The wind
Crowned with
Glory and might
Going into the darkest depths
To reach me
I cannot hide
You are there
You have spoken
In my
Despair
When thoughts
Were not clear
You have
Loved when
No more love
Was there
You know me

✖

42

&

You
Ever mindful
Of me
Always
Near

&

You
My breath
Spirit in me
Guide
Into
Kingdom place

&

Let me ride
With You
Under
Your wings
To see
And know
My destiny

&

43

&

I turn around
And see Your face
Upside down
I see Your
Face
Thank You

&

Living in
Anticipation
Of the next
Move of Your
Spirit in my
Spirit
I'm listening

&

Wind of
The Spirit
Sweep me
Off my feet
Caress me
I'm waiting

&

Barbara Kelly

44

❦

To see
The sea
Watch
The sun
Set
Then rise
Again
And
Ponder You
To look
Into the
Face of
The redeemed
And see You

❦

Here
Now
Forever
Present
My delight
Is in You

❦

45

❦

There is a lesson
Learned
Inside
The woman
You've become

❦

From darkness
To light
Confusion
Doubt
Replaced
With
Spirit-led
Spirit-fed
Always
Abiding
In Him
Yielding
To
The plan

❦

46

❧

I'm
Forever
Grateful
Mighty
Savior
I'm
Forever
Awed
Immovable
God
I'm lifted
To see
More
Than I
Ever dreamed
Precious Friend
My Provider
Loving You
Is paramount
In importance
To my
Existence

❧

47

❧

I'm diving in
Going beneath
The waves of
Glory
I'm soaring
High over the
Clouds
Standing on
Mountaintops
I'm rendered
Helpless
In Your presence
Once again
Realizing
You in me
Makes all things
Possible

❧

Hold me steady
In that place
Where You
Abide
Hold me steady
While I fly
All things possible
Through You

❧

48

❧

Decisions must be
Made
I know the answer
Is in You
You gratify me
With delightful
Reminders
Of how much
You love me

❧

Arrange the
Pieces of my life
Quiet the
Stirring of my soul
Gentle Savior
Use me

❧

By Your Spirit
I am
By Your Spirit
I will

❧

49

❧

As we put ourselves
In agreement
With You
Power is released
For You to
Bombard us
With Heaven's
Plan
To quicken us
With the nearness
Of You
We respond only
To Your voice
Act only by
Your direction
Speak
Savior
We will listen

❧

50

∽

With gratitude
I come to
Thank You
For remembered
Miracles
For answered
Prayers
For redemption
For deliverance
From the pit
Of destruction
For all You are
Doing this moment
To fulfill Your
Word
In me
Through me
For Your
Glory

∽

51

∽

When I think
There is no
More hope
You come
When I have
No more strength
You come
When I think
I am worthless
And confused
You come
Thank You

∽

Reveal what
You are devising
For us in Your
Kingdom
Open our eyes
To see
Our ears
To hear
Our minds
To receive
Wisdom

∽

Barbara Kelly

52

❧

Guidance in
This stressful
Time
Tiredness
Threatens
Weakness of
Mind and body
Warring with
Holy health
My spirit says
I'm healed
Prospered
Always welcome
In Your presence
Your place, under
Your wings
Restore
Refresh
Revive
Renew

❧

53

❧

Do I really care
What others think
There's a cacophony
Surrounding me
Center my thoughts
As I focus on You

❧

It's a God day
My eyes are focused
On Your lovely face
I've dipped into
The treasure within
Pulling up the gems
Of greatest wealth
Let me see deeper
With eyes of purity
Hope without
Doubt to interfere

❧

Fling me out there
To do the God thing
On this God day

❧

54

∽

Purposeless my
Pen
Creates a word
My mind is
Cluttered
Free me

∽

Bowing to obedience
I'll continue
In the quest
To make
Sense of
This calling

∽

It's You, LORD
Not me
Consciously I
Surrender

∽

55

∽

Guide me into Grace
While I stumble into
Forgiveness
I'm seeking
Mercy and
Serenity

∽

Overcome my shallow self
I beseech You

∽

Let Deep call to
Deep and be
My Fortress
Oh blessed
Savior
I hunger and
Thirst
Fill me

∽

Barbara Kelly

56

∽

There's a tear in
The fabric
That can only
Be repaired
By a return to
You
Help us
Not to look at
The tear
See only
You

∽

Thank You
For hearing
Thank You
For responding

∽

57

∽

A beautiful world
Created by man's
Creative mind
A soliloquy in
Rhyme

∽

A beautiful life
Created by God's
Creative design
Is a much
More desirable
Way

∽

I yield to the
God of life
Not my own
Sense of what
Is
Let it be
Don't let me
Be seen
Only You

∽

58

The day of the LORD
Is at hand
He upholds me
With His victorious
Right hand

The day of the LORD
Is at hand
Lands will tremble
Warring men
Will stumble
Life will be
Barren
For those who
Do not regard
The mighty
Right hand
Of the LORD

59

Hope deferred
Makes the
Heart sick
Hope is the legacy of
God
Who gives
A hopeful
Future

A fine jewel
Has no
Comparison
To the Pearl
Of Great Price

Honey combs
Pale in comparison
To my Savior
Much sweeter

Barbara Kelly

60

❧

They all wish
I were dead
I am a threat
To their
Unstable
Fruitless ways

❧

I wish they
Would live
As testament
To Your
Bountiful
Ways

❧

You do not
Want
Any
To Perish
But for
All
To Receive
Abundant Life

❧

61

❧

That land of
Milk and honey
Awaits me
Just over the hill
Beyond the
Mountain

❧

Am I swimming
Too fast
Too slow
Can I see
The blueprint
Please

❧

I seem dull
Of mind
And
Body

❧

Regard me
With mercy
And
Show me

❧

62

&

Determination
Will win out
I do not
Give way
To my enemy
Or listen to
The bogus
Report
I believe
The report
Of
The LORD

&

Let God arise
And
His enemies
Be
Scattered

&

63

&

I'm alarmed
As the alarm
Alarms
I'm befuddled
When sleep
Is short

&

Clear the
Cobwebs
Heavenly Father

&

Restore a
Mind full
Of
Witty ideas

&

Redeem me
Once again
As I take
Shelter
Under Your
Wings

&

Barbara Kelly

64

꿈

A quickened spirit
Is in league
With You
What a
Stunning
Union

꿈

Nothing
Is impossible
While I walk
With You
In harmony

꿈

Unravel the
Tangled
Issues
Of
Life
Make the
Paths
Straight

꿈

65

꿈

It's a sunny day
In paradise
Oh how I love
Paradise
And sunny days
There
Not here
Sunny days are
Too bright
The sand too cold
My body too weary
Transport me
To the beautiful
Place
Where all is
Perfection
A reflection
Of You

꿈

66

❧

Daughter of Jerusalem
Heed My call
Listen while I
Tell You how My
Plan for You
Will be fulfilled

❧

You will see through
A stranger's eyes
How much
Worth You have
What a treasure
I have put
Within
What I have shown
You already
Will come together
With what I
Show You now
To culminate into
The clear path of Your destiny

❧

67

❧

The wind of My
Spirit is moving
Across the minds
And hearts of
My people
To empower
Them
In these times
To translate
Through all
Barriers
To complete
My work
In the earth
Be ready
I'm coming

❧

68

❧

I wish not to be
Disillusioned
You are true
Everything else
Is false
Your will be
Accomplished
In our land
In our government
In our hearts

❧

69

❧

Forbearance
Requires
Stable minds
Attuned to
The Spirit
Not allowing
Frivolous
Interactions
That interfere

❧

A mind set like
A flint
Is controlled by
The Spirit
Not the flesh

❧

70

❧

At times I see You in
All I do
Then
At times
I see a different me
With selfish
Intent
Only moved by my
Own voice
Again I ask
Not to hear a
Stranger's voice
Not even mine

❧

71

❧

A day so wonderful
That excludes You
Cannot be compared
With being in
Your presence

❧

Today Father
Be with me
In me
Through me
To actually
Do Your will
So that my
Soul prospers

❧

72

❧

Let there be joy
In the camp
I've come back
I bring good
News
My feet are shod
With it
The news is Jesus
Saves, heals, delivers
I know Him
Therefore, I can
Say
Joy in the camp
He is here

❧

73

❧

In hues of You
Are unending
Rainbows
Sparkling stars
Graphic designs
Of grandeur
Poetic phrase and
No lack of beauty

❧

The blue-green sea
Birds in flight
Trees bowed down
All in hues of
You

❧

74

❧

Reflecting on my life
I see You have
Allowed me to be
Myself
Even stood by while
I reaped rewards
Of bad decisions
You were there to
Pick me up
What kind of
Holiness is near
The fire of my
Foolishness and
Does not get
Burned
Who are You to
Love me so

❧

75

❧

Whiling away
On the wings of
A promise
Seems fruitless
Yet
Holds the mysteries
Of the universe

❧

Ponder this

❧

Those who do not
Seek the promises

❧

Are blinded and
Wading in
The chaos of
Darkness

❧

Barbara Kelly

76

❧

Somewhere deep
Is a quiet Harmony
Wishing to be
Expressed

❧

Unfold
Sweet Harmony
Tell me
What You
Have to say

❧

You billow up
To touch my
Heart, my
Spirit soars

❧

I Am

❧

77

❧

Where do I live
Among the cliché of
Legal bondage

❧

In the blessing of
Grace
Am I filled with
Wrong thinking
Blinded by a
World
That doesn't care

❧

How do I know
Lack of the fruit of
Your spirit
Will leave me
Unaccomplished in
The desires of
Your heart

❧

Single-mindedness
Says
I will never know
Another You
Prevail
Highest of all

❧

78

❧

Savoring
Moments
Spent with You

❧

Before I arise in
The morning
You touch my
Being
I am at Peace

❧

The lingering presence
Of You brings
A longing
To hear Your voice
Thankfully
You are instantly moved
To listen
When my voice
Turns to You

❧

79

❧

Every time
I come this far
There is a
Hill to climb
When at the top
I touch You
Hear You
And know
The words
To speak

❧

No other voice
So sweet and
Strong
So compelling
Urges me
To do the
Thing You
Have called
Me to do

❧

80

❦

How to say
Thank You

❦

How to make
The world
See You

❦

How to walk
In Your footprints
Without staggering

❦

How to yield mouth
Heart and spirit
So that the world
Knows
How excellent it is
To know
You
In all Your fullness

❦

81

❦

Your tragedy
Holds me
To a chord
Between You
Me, and God
That cannot
Be broken

❦

Rest, assured
That He hears
Me when
I lift you
Before Him
In Love

❦

His Love is
Instant
Complete
Infallible
Pure and
Everlasting
Toward You
Be at Peace

❦

82

❦

Lasting
Friendships
Are rare
When
Elevated
To a higher
Level
With You
As
The common
Denominator

❦

We become
Family
With You
And
One another

❦

We are truly
Treasures
In an earthen
Vessel

❦

83

❦

You are precious
Sweet daughter
Friend

❦

Heed the higher
Call
Express
God Within

❦

Come to grips
With
Forgiveness

❦

Learn to fly

❦

84

≈

When its You
The way is clear
The plan, complete

≈

When it's me
The way is erratic

≈

Looking through
A clouded glass

≈

I want You
Your plan
To encroach
On the flesh and
Clean the glass

≈

85

≈

No further discussion
Will help me understand
You better
Swing down please
To my height
Touch these yearnings
To hear what You
Say

≈

Tell the world where You
live
I'm real
I want to communicate
With each of them
Set them on higher ground
Hear their need
Answer their desires
Redeem them for all eternity
From the curse of the law
To bring life and blessing
Each day here on earth
And for all eternity.

≈

86

✺

I am Love
I respond to
Those who need
This love

✺

I am the shelter in
A storm
For these who need a
Port for rest

✺

I am the father
To an orphaned world

✺

I am the answer to
Questions that astound
Scholars

✺

Seek Me and
Find Me
Wherever You
Have a need

✺

I Am
Will be on Your side

✺

87

✺

These lofty ideas
Of who I am
Come from You

✺

From our years
Of conversation

✺

Create in me knowledge
Of how to interpret
What You are
Saying to me

✺

I'm hungering and
Thirsting
After Your righteousness

✺

I, Your child of Zion
Respond to this
Unction

✺

Barbara Kelly

88

❧

Shadows over the water
Say You are near
Troubling the water

❧

So I can dip my
Lameness in

❧

This cup of oil
You hand me
Is running over
To drown me
In Your Spirit

❧

This flutter of wings
Rushing past me
To show You are
Mindful of my need
For Protection and
Ministry

❧

The Blood I feel pumping
In my veins
Assures me
I am born of blood and water
An enormous gift

❧

89

❧

Illumination
Is present
To dispel
Darkness
To show clearly
What You say

❧

The undertaker
Digs a big hole
You shine Your
Light
I am reprieved

❧

Flesh says I need
More of all the
World presents

❧

You give light
To those things
That enhance
Not take away

❧

Light of God
Shine on

❧

90

᠕

The oracles of God
Go deep
As the deep-blue sea

᠕

Put on Your diving gear
Go down
Receive all
There is
At the depth

᠕

Bring it to the top
To feed the
Multitude

᠕

Then dive again
Until they
Are all fed
And
Time is no more

᠕

91

᠕

The sparsity of
Interest
Would drown
My enthusiasm

᠕

Except You and I
Have such a
Good time
Visiting

᠕

All else seems
Sublime

᠕

Barbara Kelly

92

⁊

Do these distractions
Deter You
No
They move me
To a less
Admirable state

⁊

There's no high road
In sickness, disease
And infirmity
No hope is there

⁊

The power of God
Within
Rescues me
From
These
Distractions
Gives me authority
To command the
Truth to prevail

⁊

93

⁊

I prefer spending
Time with
A precious few

⁊

Those who lift me
Up to You

⁊

In perilous times
There's no Grace
Like Yours

⁊

In elevated times of
Celebration
There's no greater
Purpose than to
Sing Your praises

⁊

94

❧

To arrive on time
Is to listen to
Your voice in
The still of the
Moment
Allowing Your
Spirit
To guide me
Into the worlds
Beyond
With no time or
Space
Ages of eternity
Are here now

❧

95

❧

No to the
Suggestions of
Despair
No
To the hopelessness
Of a day on
Earth
Yes
To the One who
Sings over me
And
Promises to hide
Me under His wings
Yes to the call from
Alpha and Omega
Yes
I cry
To the One
Who loves me

❧

Barbara Kelly

96

≪

Unending welcome
Of magnificent
Proportions

≪

Prevails
In the house of
The LORD

≪

In the domain of
The King
Who is my Father

≪

I exist

≪

97

≪

Assuming the worst
Confirms Satan's
Ultimate goal

≪

Attesting to the best
Confirms God's
Phenomenal plan
To exonerate
From all evil
Replaced by
Peace Joy
Forgiveness
Forgetting all that
Was

≪

Today is not too
Late to step into
Mercy and be
Forgiven

≪

98

❧

Your very gaze
Is charged
With Love
Your thoughts
Produce real-time
Action
Your presence
Reduces all other
Spirits
To dust

❧

And now
The best is yet
To come

❧

In the meantime
I have Power
Dominion, Grace
And
Mercy at work
In me
Now

❧

99

❧

However tall the
Tree grows
Its grace is
Unmatched

❧

Nothing shines
Like
The Son

❧

No darkness
As complete
As one second
Without Him

❧

Barbara Kelly

100

❧

Is there a
Prayer
For
A
Hungry
Soul
That
Will Not
Be answered

❧

Does my
Supposed
Importance
Redeem me

❧

Will the roll
Call
Come with my
Name missing

❧

Hallelujah
I am
Saved

❧

101

❧

While I yield
My plan to
Yours I have
Straight A's
No failure

❧

Forgiveness
Is quick

❧

All is well
In the
House of
The Lord

❧

102

❧

Minimal
Requirement
To assemble

❧

The children
Of God
When the
Father calls

❧

Bring only
You
Sit beneath
His wings

❧

He does the
Rest

❧

My only
Requirement
Lean heavy
And
Trust

❧

103

❧

Sweet announcement
Coming from
Your bosom

❧

That we are
Entitled to be
Enfolded in
The
The Great
I Am

❧

To only observe
The ways
You change
Situations
Send out angels
Deliver
The ultimatum
To the wicked

❧

Barbara Kelly

104

❧

I'm enmeshed
In the anointing
You place

❧

In the place
I am
In the connections You make

❧

That I may
Show
Your
Infinity of
Love and Grace
To the needy

❧

105

❧

Twisted fate
Cannot happen
When
Enfolded
In
The magnificence
Of
The kingdom
The expected
Is always
The unexpected
By the
Flow of Your
Spirit

❧

106

In the midst of
All I know
Is all
I don't know

What joy to
Know
That
You know
All
And
You impart
What I need
If my ears
And
Eyes
Are filled
With You

107

There's a
Need in me
To
Live
Love
Laugh
And
Be happy

Holy Father
Please come
To this
Celebration
Of
The promise
Of
All highest
Dimensions
Fulfilled

Barbara Kelly

108

❧

Whatever
Ghosts
Assume
To
Infringe
On my
Peace
Are
Thankfully
Apparitions
With no
Importance
And
No substance

❧

109

Part One

❧

Did You
Live
To see me
Die
Or
Die
To see me
Live

❧

Did You know
I would
Come
Along
With
Failure
Written
On
Every Plan
Is that
Why
You
Said
The best-laid
Plans

❧

110

Part Two

ર્સ

Were of no
Importance
Without
You
Then reached
Down
In my
Despair
To Love
Me
Anyway

ર્સ

To straighten
Out my
Crooked
Paths
Thank You
Lover
Of
My soul

ર્સ

111

ર્સ

Sweeten
The pot
So that
When I
Eat
The
Outpouring
Of
My
Heart
Will
Sound
Like
You

ર્સ

Barbara Kelly

112

❧

Expand
This
Moment
Of
Time
To
Reveal
The
Set time

❧

Let the
Years
Leap
Forward
For
Us
All

❧

113

❧

Half and half
You came
And
Whole
You went

❧

Whole
You return
To come
For the
Ones
You
Made whole

❧

I am
A witness
To
This conversion

❧

114

✧

Surrounded
By
Sights and
Sounds
Combining
To
Make
Confusion

✧

Focus
Is
To
Never
See or
Hear
Without
Heaven's
View

✧

115

✧

Some
Say
It's a
Rude
Awakening

✧

I
Say
It's
A
Beautiful
View
When
Walls
Crumble
Demons
Scatter

✧

Barbara Kelly

116

❧

The History Maker
Lives in me
While my intentions
Wander
Into
Worlds of my own
Making
He unravels the
Tangled mess
Walks into
My spirit
With His
Tender ways
Saying
Come

❧

117

❧

Today is more
Significant
In the
Unfolding
Of Your plan
Than ever
Before

❧

I'm glad to
Remove old
Tapes
Old
Behavior
Old
Reasons
Not
To move
Forward
With You

❧

118

❧

In sweetness
You arrive
To touch
Me
With You
And Your
Infinite Love

❧

Oh
Gracious Father
That I always
Entertain You
Is my desire

❧

What triumph
Fills my heart just
To know You

❧

119

❧

It's the strangest
Thing
To think
I could be
A wilder
Rendition
Of me and
Not forsake
The call
Walk into
The Grace
Overtaken
By
Your majesty

❧

Barbara Kelly

120

❦

Red shoes
Smooth jazz
A day
Without
Trauma
A
Singularly
Pleasant
Reminder
Of
Your favor
In my
Otherwise
Effervescent
Life

❦

121

❦

Savoring a
Moment in
Time
Perfect
For me
With
A plan
A destiny
In this
Moment of
Time
I walk
Not run
So to
Listen
Savoring
You

❦

122

❧

I see through
The mist of time
A lovely
View
No despair
A more
Fluent
Passage
Into
The place

❧

123

❧

To
Combine
With
You
In this
Collaboration
Transcends
Normal
Life

❧

Powerful
Emissions
Come
Through
This
Union

❧

None so wise
None so eager
To speak
And have
Listeners

❧

Barbara Kelly

124

❧

I
Welcome
You
To
Walk
Through
The
Passages
Of
My mind

❧

To
Break
Sound
Barriers

❧

To
Enter
This
Body of
Flesh
For the
Release of
Power
To deliver and heal

❧

125

❧

Sweeter than
The
Honeycomb
You
Satiate
My hunger

❧

Brighter
Far
Brighter
Than
The
Morning
Star
To light
My path

❧

More pure
Than fine
Gold
To
Embellish
My life

❧

126

❧

Whistles
Blow
So do
Trumpets

❧

A difference
In
Sound
Determines
Appropriate
Action

❧

Be ready
For
The trumpet

❧

127

❧

Wherever my
Voice
Goes
Let it speak
Of
You
Wherever
My
Feet go
Good News
Is spread

❧

Whatever
My hands
Do
Prospers

❧

Holy One
Remain

❧

Barbara Kelly

128

❧

Arise
Passionate
One

❧

Teach me
How to
Reach
Higher
Into the
Heavens

❧

Until there
Is no
Space
Between
For
Falling

❧

129

❧

Windswept
I crept
Beneath
Covers
To call
Upon Your
Majesty to
Hold me
I commissioned
Your Spirit
To comfort
Slept in
Peace
Only You
Can give
Awakened to
Find
You
Had
Sustained
Me
What a treasure
You are
Lord of Hosts

❧

130

❧

You never
Leave
Anyone

❧

We are the
One's to
Leave

❧

No more
Tender
Father
Could
I have

❧

Not a condemning
Spirit
Nor a
Condemning
Word

❧

Even Your
Reproof
Is
Respectful to
Your child

❧

131

❧

I clamor
For time
As it slips
Through my
Fingers

❧

Wow,I turn
Over these
Trickling
Cascades of
Time
To You

❧

There is an
Abundance

❧

You
Amaze
Me

❧

Barbara Kelly

132

❧

Nothing
Stands
When
You
Speak

❧

All
Creation
Responds

❧

Every
Name
Named
Under
Heaven
Bows

❧

Give us
A clearer
Unfettered
View
Of
You

❧

133

❧

Laying
Down
My
Human
Preferences

❧

I accept
Your
Way

❧

What
A beautiful
Seamless
Path

❧

Without
Distress
And
Focused

❧

134

❧

Live
Big
In
This
Temple

❧

Expand
My
Tent
Stakes

❧

Free
My
Curtains

❧

Let the
Wind
Blow
And
Clear
The
Cobwebs

❧

135

❧

I've
Been
Released
The
Blessing
Now flows

❧

Not charity
From
The
Earthly
Realm
A
Royal
Flow
From
The window
Of
Heaven
I'm free

❧

Barbara Kelly

136

❧

Watching
Believing

❧

Never
Switching
Sides

❧

Hearing
The
Wind
Sweeping
A
Wide
Path
Of
Healing
Prospering
Deliverance
From
Heaven

❧

137

❧

When
I
Am
Seen

❧

It's
You

❧

For those
Who
Hunger
And
Thirst
After
Righteousness

❧

I'm
The
Only
View
Of
You

❧

138

❧

Winter
Has
Subsided
The
Buds
Burst
Out of
The
Cracks
About
To
Be
Released into
Full
Blown
Splendor

❧

The earth
Rejoices

❧

139

❧

Seeing eyes
Hearing ears
Are not
Hindered
They run
Not walk

❧

To the
Untold
Glory
Of the
Manifest
God
Who
Reigns
On
A
Throne
A
White horse
A
Cloud

❧

140

❧

Your Word
Is so
Important
That
You
Honor it
With Your
Presence
There is
Life-giving
Power
To reveal
You
Who You
Really
Want us
To see

❧

Praise be
To God
Who shows
Himself strong
In my
Behalf

❧

141

❧

In the court of
Heaven
Trumped up
Charges against
God's children
Are defeated

❧

Allegations of
Grandeur by
Others
Will not stand

❧

False doctrine
May register
In deceived
Hearts

❧

No hope is
Found there

❧

Praise to the
God of the
Universe

❧

142

❧

You became
Holiness
Incarnate

❧

Never
Wavering
Or
Falling out
Of step

❧

You
Conquered

❧

Now I'm
A conqueror
Through
My
Blessed
Savior

❧

Praise be
To
The Holy
God

❧

143

❧

A paradox
To be a human
With the Spirit
Of Almighty God
Living within

❧

Unhindered
I speak
Yet
Not me
But the
Holy One

❧

Why me

❧

I am
Willing and
Satisfied
When
Yielding to
You

❧

Barbara Kelly

144

❧

A whimper in
The darkness
Another soul
Undone

❧

While time
Marches on

❧

No one seems
To care

❧

Then You send
Angels to
Impart
Divine Love
And
Deliverance
From the
Evil One

❧

Another soul
Is found

❧

Eternity wins

❧

145

❧

Rejected
Not in
A comely form

❧

The dance
Continues between
The Trinity and
Man

❧

Trinity steps
Up to take
The lead

❧

When enlightened
Man
Says
Yes

❧

146

❦

Nothing ventured
Nothing gained

❦

Without You
All my ventures
Would fall
Flat

❦

I've ventured and
I've gained
A true God
A Wonderful Friend
A hope and a future
Without end

❦

You sing over me
And dance about wildly

❦

Just because I'm Your
Child

❦

Let me be pleasing
To You today

❦

147

❦

Whatever happened
To my ostensibly

❦

Creative mind
Have I lost
My mind or
Just the creativity

❦

Sometimes the effort
To remain
Grows even
Harder than
To
Rock on to
The next stop

❦

Barbara Kelly

148

❧

Sincerity
Plus
God's plan
Equals a

❧

Wonderful
Relationship

❧

That will not
Fail

❧

He makes the
Darkened path
Plain and

❧

Sings a song
Of
Rejoicing

❧

149

❧

Arising from
Sunshine
Walking in
Dewy grass

❧

I slip into a
Dream of a
Beautiful
Home
Designed by
God
To gratify
My
Longing to
Be a
Blessing to
Many who
Suffer or
Do not have
The knowledge
Of
You

❧

150

❧

The winter
Has past
My heart
Sings
For the
New birth
Of
All I see

❧

Come into the
Morning of
My life and
Remain until
The Son
Comes down

❧

We will all
Be Your army
Enlisted by
God
To bring slaves
Of
Satan to the
Sweet understanding
Of all You are

❧

151

❧

The Witness is
In me
The Witness
Remains

❧

Pillars fall
Sound ceases

❧

A ripe spirit
Produces a
Bountiful
Fruit

❧

An open mind
Must be renewed
Or
Many false
Prophets with
False ideas
Will result

❧

I am rich and
Supplanted to the
Highest Power

❧

Barbara Kelly

152

❧

The Goodness of
God
Overwhelms me

❧

How to express
How much
His Love
Has transformed
My life here
And my choice
For eternity

❧

There is nothing
Worthwhile in
Me
Only You

❧

Lift darkness
From my
Eyes
Open my ears

❧

Let Wisdom have
Her perfect plan

❧

153

❧

Where there is
A need
Step in
Through me
Undo
Hurt

❧

Cause the Mighty
Arm of God to
Strip the enemy
And
Release the
Captives

❧

Create a new
Heart to view
You
To be
A resting place
For the
Weary is my
Desire

❧

154

∽

Have I seen
The best
Or
Is it still to come

∽

Why settle for
Indiscriminate
Mindless belief
Following in
A crowd who
Is not sure why
No one is
In charge
That exhibits
Anything but
Hate

∽

155

∽

For Your sake
For my sake
I will obey
The holiness
Within
Only by Your
Hand
Will my flesh
Subside

∽

My hope is in
You not my
Feeble
Attempt at
Righteousness

∽

Barbara Kelly

156

☙

Sweeping
Sensations
Are washing
Over my
Soul
No more days
Without cause

☙

How to tell You of
My irrational
Nonproductive
Meanderings

☙

Whitewashed
Lies
Promote this temple
Not
Your Highness

☙

157

☙

I love the
Camaraderie with
You
To know You
Never see me
In despair
Rather
With a Divine
Purpose
No time is lost
When I surrender
The
Obstinate will of
My uncrucified
Flesh
To the Holy One
Who
Loves me
Unconditionally

☙

158

❧

Unlimited resources
Are in my possession
Where can I go
But
To the LORD

❧

Efficiency of
Purpose
Calamity of
Soul
Brings Salvation
To the surface

❧

This conquering
Force is

❧

The Overcomer

❧

159

❧

More time than
Money
Is the saying

❧

More of You
Less of me

❧

Money overtakes
Time

❧

The grim reaper
Is swallowed
In the Life-
Giver

❧

Barbara Kelly

160

❧

Sweeter than
The aroma
Of my finest
Choice
Is the presence of
The fragrance of
You

❧

A beauty unmatched
Cannot be bought
Over the counter

❧

A love so pure
And undefiled
With no relation
To my love

❧

161

❧

You walked among
Them and they
Did not know

❧

Today I walk
Among them
With You

❧

Believing
They
Will know

❧

162

❧

The winner's circle is
Comprised of many who
Have yielded
Their strength and
Position to
The God of Glory

❧

My hope comes from
Above
Without wavering

❧

No further knowledge
Convinces me
Otherwise

❧

163

❧

Awaken the dead
In Christ
That the Holy Spirit
Can be
Recognized

❧

By their fruits
We shall know
Them

❧

Let the dry bones
Come to life
Becoming a
Witness to
The power
Of
God

❧

The beauty of God
Will cover the land
Rivers will flow
Flowers bloom

❧

There will be dancing
In the streets

❧

Barbara Kelly

164

❦

There is a Will that
Walks the earth

❦

I have no union with
Another

❦

This Will is a
Documentary to
Heaven's design
For me

❦

I can see no other
Plan but
Thee

❦

165

❦

Sweeter than my
Sweetest memories is
Your presence

❦

Don't think I'm weak
Or
Lacking intelligence

❦

All I am is ruled by
I Am

❦

None can compare to
His greatness

❦

Yet
He calls me by
Name
He knows my voice

❦

166

❦

I crumble in the
Face of adversity
Like
Humpty dumpty off
The wall

❦

However
I serve the One
Who picks up the
Pieces of
My life
So that I'm
Better
Than before

❦

He cares for
Me

❦

167

❦

Starburst
Moonshine
Colored rainbows
Are
Hallowed
By some

❦

My God
Rides on the clouds
Sends
Rainbows as a
Promise

❦

Places a star to
Guide
The wise

❦

Gives the moon to
Light
The darkness and
Watches me
Day and night

❦

Barbara Kelly

168

᪉

Forever in my
Memory

᪉

A reflection of
You

᪉

All You have
Invested in me

᪉

Why I rest in
You

᪉

The mystery of
Reciprocity

᪉

The way You
Promise to
Keep Your

᪉

Promises

᪉

How do I ever
Forget the One
Who occupies
My current
Memories
My past
Redeemed
My future
Security

᪉

169

᪉

A treasured
Indulgence

᪉

The ways You
Show up
Making Your
Approval known
To my spirit

᪉

I'm never alone
Or
Without words to
Express my
Devotion to
You

᪉

The choices
Are so much
Easier
When
Your wisdom
Enters a
Crowded mind

᪉

How do I express
My gratitude

᪉

170

❧

A stronger approach
A definite response

❧

When hell encounters
My wrath

❧

Knowing
My latitude has
Expired

❧

My Heaven backs

❧

All I pour out in

❧

The name of Jesus

❧

The autumn of my
Life is
Expressed by

❧

Your gifts within

❧

Come
Greater One
In me

❧

Come

❧

171

❧

Illiterate soul

❧

Bow Your knee

❧

To the name

❧

Of Jesus

❧

Worldly mind
Come under
Subjection to
The mind of
God
Body of flesh

❧

Be reminded

❧

You are the temple

❧

Barbara Kelly

172

❧

As the periphery of
My life
Moves further away
My vision clears

❧

The Lover of my
Soul speaks
I hear

❧

He shows Himself
So strong and
Beautiful in my
Behalf

❧

How could I look
Elsewhere

❧

173

❧

Extreme measures
Have been taken to
Separate
The wheat from

❧

The chaff

❧

The oil has
Been poured
Sweet wine
Accompanies

❧

The chosen
Remnant
Remains

❧

174

❧

Exquisite reminder

❧

The smothering
Spirit doesn't

❧

Have a place to

❧

Hide all the results

❧

Of His torture

❧

We are
Overcomers

❧

In the midst of a

❧

Harmonious

❧

Battle with one

❧

Already defeated

❧

The Light

❧

Prevails

❧

With tortured

❧

Ones released

❧

Barbara Kelly

❧

Swifter than you
Know
I'm registering
The many
Coming to Me
My set time
Is now
Keep alert to
My presence

❧

You are surrounded by
My angels

❧

They will not, I say
Will not
Allow you to be
Destroyed

❧

Even now they are
Doing battle for you

❧

Lifting up your
Tired body

❧

Bringing to pass *all*

❧

I have called you to

❧

In the earlier days

❧

❧

I walk into this day
Armoured
Favored
Blessed coming in
Going out
Anointed to prosper
Anointed to peace

❧

I am gifted
Chosen
Always in Your presence

❧

Have Your way, Dear One
Prompt me
Arrange the pages of
My life
You are honored
I am Yours

❧

177

❧

Admission has a price
You paid
I didn't

❧

The show is
Everlasting
A one-time deal

❧

I am robed and
Crowned
Awaiting my
Chariot

❧

Never late
Never early

❧

The show is
About to begin

❧

178

❧

Did you ever notice
How soft He speaks
When a thunderous
Retort would be our
Due

❧

How does the God
Of all creation who
Is and ever was
The Beginning and
The End
Talk to me in language
I understand

❧

Savoring His presence
In a quiet moment
Or
When all hell is battering
He is the Sufficient One
To meet every one
Of my needs
He sees my heart and
Loves me

❧

Barbara Kelly

179

❧

Compliance with
Your will
Sets me free
To walk
Circumspectly
Knowing
You are at the
Helm
Parting the
Waters
Leveling rocky
Ground
Lifting my
Feet to fly
As Deep calls unto
Deep

❧

180

❧

Workers of iniquity
Settle in
Dark places
The untold acts
Of this darkness
Cannot overpower
The Lght

❧

I'm pushing against
The goads
The pain is too great
Release me I
Command
I'll walk within Your
Tender care

❧

181

❧

The sumptuousness of
This supper set
Before me is a
Rendering of Heaven's
Promise
The gold and crystal
Are a testimony of
God's Holy Word

❧

Rivers of oil flow
From my cup
It indeed
Runneth over

❧

I savor this time
Of my history while
My Savior says
Come home

❧

Oh that my eyes
May see Thy Glory

❧

182

❧

It's the wholesomeness of
You that draws me
Into a place I've
Never been

❧

I'm guided by a Lamp
Upon my feet and
A Light unto my path

❧

Christians behold
There is no comfort in
Trite remembrance or
Repeated sing-song
Moves trying to capture
An audience

❧

There is comfort in
Knowing the One who
Created you, knows you
Intimately
Craves Your company
Turns a simple day
Into an exotic
Experience

❧

Barbara Kelly

183

❧

Commonly known as
Writer's block
It's actually a matter of
The Spirit

❧

Come in all Your wisdom and
Unique view
Occupy my senses

❧

Block out the elevation
Of man so that I
May hear, see, touch,
Feel the omniscience
In ways that my
Heart only
Can repeat the
Eloquence

❧

184

❧

This work must be
Seen
To gather to You
The hearts of men

❧

Let this be my last
Legacy to the ones
Left behind

❧

My days are in Your
Hands
My reward is in
Knowing You
With me
Brings this to pass

❧

Let the work of my hands
Be prospered
In order not to need
Anything and to be
Thoroughly furnished
Unto all good works

❧

Pause and calmly
Think on this

❧

185

&

I bless You with
My hands
I bless You with my
Words and my heart
When I think of the
Limitations of my
Development
Without You
I am ashamed to
Think I could ever
Succeed without
Surrender
For You to so desire
My well-being
In all areas is
More than I can
Comprehend with
My finite mind

&

Arise in me
Spirit of The Living God
And
Speak

&

186

&

If the price is reduced
Is the quality the same

&

I think not

&

The price was high and
Paid by Heaven's only
Son
No other price is sufficient

&

Surely, You say
I can pay a lesser
Price if the result is
The same

&

You do not see the Truth
You cannot buy at any
Price what has already
Been accomplished
It's a done deal
Please
Accept The Gift without
Reduced quality
No further price paid

&

Barbara Kelly

187

❧

A sign has been given
The response was
Great
Renowned by Heaven
And kings

❧

The worship was
Inspired by prophets
Renderings

❧

I continue in the parade of
Worshipers
Who are looking for
A new sign
A new trumpet
A Savior who always
Existed and will always
Be
My anticipation is
Escalating

❧

188

❧

You complement me with
All things good

❧

You arrive on time
Never empty-handed

❧

You are a welcome
Intrusion on my
Mundane life

❧

Have You ever turned a
Deaf ear to Your child
Have I ever turned a
Deaf ear to You

❧

How I have neglected You
Yet You never fail

❧

189

∽

You comfort me with
Good things
Not evil

∽

The uprising of my
Soul causes me to
Soar above the earthly
And
See as You see

∽

Don't ever leave
Keep prodding me
Forward
I must have
More

∽

190

∽

The convenience plan
Lets me enjoy without
Payment until later

∽

The convenience of Your
Plan is I enjoy now and
Always
Without ever paying

∽

I toil not but
I am made rich
My rich Father is ever
Mindful of my needs
He even delights in me
He gives me the desires of
My heart
The ones He put in there
What a good Father
What a powerful God
Who has redeemed me and
Made me His child

191

࿔

Living in a dead heat
Against time
While eternity's clock
Keeps ticking

࿔

Times will soon soon
Cease
My race will give way
To victory everlasting
There is no greater
Trophy for a race
Well run than to
Live forever in
Your heavenly place
Basking in You

࿔

192

࿔

If there's a conscious
Effort on my part

࿔

There's a corresponding
Blessing to empower
Me in all areas
You awaken my
Mind and body to
Prosper and to give
Spiritually, financially, as
Well as from a
Compassionate heart

࿔

Love of my life
Compliment my efforts
With Your Spirit
Renderings

࿔

How truly great
Thou art

࿔

193

❦

The uncommon Truth is
The common reality
The Truth has set me
Free
To walk unfettered
To see with spiritual eyes
To behold Your majesty
What other inspiration is
Necessary
What Truth but this must
I know

❦

194

❦

Up the down staircase
Winding road
Going nowhere
Slip-sliding in
Reckless abandon
A worthless adventure

❦

I whiplash a turn
To see the other road
The abandon is peace
The moving staircase
Removes my efforts

❦

This adventure leads to
Higher ground

❦

Barbara Kelly

195

≈

Pearl of Great Price
Adorn me
Rose of Sharon
Let me breathe Your
Sweet fragrance

≈

Incense of Heaven
Calm my shattered
Nerves

≈

Holy Communion
Be my portion
While I ride on
Blissful waves and
Summon my strength
From Your joy

≈

196

≈

Lifter of my head

≈

I hear the melody
You sing
Your dance is
Beautiful

≈

Your raiment
Glows with the
Essence of You

≈

Fill my senses

≈

197

❧

Even a whisper from
You is louder than
A human voice
The rendering much
Swifter to tear down
Strongholds
Give heightened
Wisdom
Create a world and
All that's in it
That whisper is what
I hear and not the
Voice of a stranger

❧

198

❧

Flamboyance is my
Style
Not the bland of a
Timid life

❧

I've noticed Your
Flamboyance in
Stars
Moon
Sun
The awesomeness of
Blue-capped mountains
Regal birds
Intricately designed
Animals

❧

All for me to enjoy
Endlessly

❧

I long to witness the
Breathless view of
Heaven's bounty

❧

Barbara Kelly

199

❧

Wanderlust takes over in
Spring
The countless ways to
Unwind in summer

❧

Outdoors in fall becomes
My living room
The snow of winter brings
A wonderland to enhance
The imagination

❧

Why do I stay dormant
When all is changing so
Fast around me

❧

Help me to keep up

❧

200

❧

A weeping willow
In a shrouded
Garden
Envelops God's world
With timelessness
To witness all
The many wonders
Of this majesty

❧

Birds nest there
Next to sizeable
Animals
No contest
All is Peace and
Beauty
I am at rest

❧

201

≪

If I could wish upon
A star and fly over
Rafters
Twitch my nose to
Change the scene or
Level the devil with a
Glance
I wouldn't need a
Savior or His Spirit
In me to perform
God's radical renewal
Release from Satan's
Grasp and by His
Authority exchange
My home to the one
He has prepared

≪

202

≪

Sweet summer wind
In swaying treetops
Waves lapping on
The beach
Doves resting in a
Nearby limb
All reduce me to
See my humanity
And
Your grandeur

≪

Barbara Kelly

203

❧

Perhaps a day
Longer will bring
The triumphant
Future You have
Planned

❧

I'm a seeker of truth
A willing participant
In this so-called
Life

❧

Without a backward
Glance
The life I've chosen
Turns into abundance
Only You could
Orchestrate

❧

204

❧

Beautiful One
May I bask in
Your loveliness

❧

I really need
Loveliness to fill
All my senses

❧

Invade my thoughts
With
How You think
So that
I am not limited
By what I know
Father

❧

Expanded by what
You know
Dropping these fetters
Becoming Godlike in
All my endeavors

❧

205

❧

A power driver of great
Magnitude
Separating
Spirit from soul
Slicing through the
Bone to get to the
Marrow
Where there is Life
Blood
To sanctify the
Body
Purify the soul and
Let the spirit reign

❧

206

❧

A deeper well could not be
Found so
You drank from one
Man devised

❧

Your thirst was not
Quenched until
Man's was

❧

Even mud at the bottom
Blessed by You is
Better than the
Purest water
Man made

❧

∽

The Spirit in me says
Awaken men to the
Truth and beauty of
You
Read what my pen
Writes
Search Your hearts
Hear the Master's
Voice calling You
To come into His
Palace of Peace
Everlasting
Walk on streets of
Gold
Witness the Great
Forever

∽

∽

Star of David
You are all the Light
Needed to
Slay these dragons and
Bears
I grow stronger now
Because the smell of
Victory in slaying
The enemy spurs
My spirit and
Intellect to higher
Ground

∽

209

❧

I'm swept into this
Secret place
Where You and I commune
Nowhere is as rich
Beautiful and full of
Sweetness

❧

Corruption is flowing
Around
Yet
You can interfere in
This
Secret place

❧

210

❧

A Holy Cloud
A rushing wind
Celebration in the air

❧

In the vortex of this
Storm
You come, Oh Holy One
Lifting my eyes to
See a view of You
My heart and all
Senses
Reveal I Am is
Near

❧

Barbara Kelly

211

❧

Pulling the chord
The bell rings
The curtain opens
To unveil
The Holy of Holies
In all His righteousness

❧

His sweet countenance of
Purest delight
Looks on me with such
Love
I cannot look elsewhere
Oh, Holy One
So divine
Lift me up
To where
You are

❧

212

❧

The merciless one has
Spoken lies
To confound the wise
To dishonor my worth
To steal the fortunes
You have laid up for
Me

❧

I am reminded of Your
All-sufficient presence
In my life to rescue
The perishing
To care for all my
Cares
To honor all Your
Benefits

❧

Sublime Father of
Mercy and
Grace

❧

Witness through me
To the distressed
. That You are
Here among us

❧

213

∽

Glorious Overcomer
Ignite that spirit in
Me
To overwhelm the
Darkness with
Power and a
Knowledge of who
I was before time
Began

∽

214

∽

My depth of perception
Sees beyond the present
Into a place of
Excellent vision
Seeing into the soul of
Man
With God-Sight

∽

Lovers of vision
Precepts of time
Before time

∽

Awakening the ever
Present You in me
To reconstruct
Thoughts
Rearrange
Patterns of life
Remove all
Sorrow and
Reestablish who is
Now and always
In control

∽

Barbara Kelly

215

᠀

Is the reflection looking
Back at me
A true embodiment of
Who I am or
Is the reflection
Merely a concept of
Who I perceive myself
To be

᠀

A vision through a vision
Resembles the Truth
The Truth has made
The way
To meet every challenge
Of
Fact

᠀

216

᠀

If there's an
Anomaly
Lingering
Research my heart
Know me
Shine Your Light
In these corners of
My mind to
Expose
Truth from fiction

᠀

217

∽

The clouds are moving
Fiercely moving

∽

Your outstretched arm
Points to the east

∽

I see the Cloud of Glory
Moving into place

∽

Come, let us drink the
Wine
Break the bread
Prepare the way
Let not one wounded
Pass without sustenance
Redemption draws nigh
Come

∽

218

∽

Stay in place
My delight is in you
Go with me to
Another realm
I'll show you the
Harvest ripe
Use you to be
Me in the land of
The living
Wipe away the tears of
Frustration
Cast off the garment of
Remorse
Become my head
Above the circumstance
I'll protect you with My
Mighty right arm
I am pointing now toward
The eastern sky

∽

Barbara Kelly

219

∾

A new day
A special time
A place I've never
Gone before
Spirit in me
Arise to this
Occasion
Tempt me not
You worker of
Iniquity
My Father is
Calling
Hear
Listen
The Word is
Clear
Obey
Walk with me
Into an abundance
You have only
Dreamed of
You are clothed in
Righteousness
A royal being from
The throne of God
Sent to destroy the
Works of the devil

∾

220

∾

It is a call to arms
The trumpet calls
The mighty army to
A battle stance
Never in the history of
Man has there been such a
Vast revolt of Heaven and
Earth to shake off the
Dross leaving a
God-established
Head
Be ready

∾

221

❧

The Knowing Spirit within
Knows my days are numbered
As the stars have been
My times are set
The moment becomes
a thousand
Moments
Removing time and space
Life as known
Recedes
Leaving a clear space to
Enter
Where my communion
Is complete

❧

222

❧

A rendezvous with
You is my invitation to
Settle into Your space
A gleeful spirit has
Me in its grip
When
I surrender
Knowing I'll be
Quick to
Respond to Your
Person
To hear only
Your voice

❧

Barbara Kelly

223

❧

The Lion and the Lamb
Are in place
The stars and moon
Contemplate a Light much
Brighter than the sun
The sun is saying
I will refuse to shine
When the Son shines
All is ready
The earth groans
The creatures are
Stirred
Look up
Oh You of little faith
Remember the One
Who formed the sky
The sun and moon
Who hung the stars and
Calls You by name

❧

224

❧

I am called to write
What You are saying

❧

Abraham was asked to
Lay down His son's life

❧

Just as God laid down
His son's life

❧

He now asks me to lay
Down my son's life

❧

Forgetting the scourge of
The past

❧

Pouring out the oil of
Anointing on his head

❧

I believe and receive
A new creation in Him
To step on the head of
The serpent
To be released from
Every lie of hell
To regard only the True
Word of the Living God

❧

225

❧

Even numbers are
Distributed
Uneven numbers
Overtake them
When the Son of Man
Arises to rule the
Whole earth
The numbers will be
Complete

❧

226

❧

There is a path with a
Fissure on each side

❧

You have shown Your
Delight of
My choice to
Be committed to the
Path and not the
Fissures
Walk on, my child
The day is to be
Seized, for the night
Is coming
My lamp will shine
In the darkness
If
You stay on the
Path

❧

Barbara Kelly

227

❧

I am ready
Time is not an issue
Money is not an issue
I curse any contrary
Spirit
Releasing the thoughts of
God over my life
Good thoughts
Not evil
Prevail

❧

Pillars stand in my defense
The red carpet is rolled out
My feet glow with the
Good News

❧

Prepare the way
Good Shepherd

❧

228

❧

I stand by the river of
Life
Tasting The Wine
Such peace in lush
Green pastures
Son of Glory
I bask in You
Sweep clean all the
Debris of my heart
Summon me
I will come

❧

229

❧

God of many facets
A never-ending flow
Of piquant thoughts
So rare is Your design
Duplicating is only a
Version of You

❧

Sublimate my desires to
One who has a vast
Store of exciting
Revelations plumbing the
Depths of my mind
Overtake me

❧

230

❧

Entice me
I exalt You
Invite You
Come dine with
Me
At this table set
Before me
A table of opulence
Oh
Heaven be present as
I partake of the
Fatted calf

❧

Barbara Kelly

231

Among the powers of the
Earth
None can change direction of
The wind
Make a life within a life
Or
Right a weary world or
Calm a storm tossed sea

Power of God, whose desire
Is the heart I expose
Reason with my
Supposition of humility
Lifting human frailty
To Honor and Royalty

232

The summation of my
Days says You are all
There is to gratify
The attempt to succeed
Were I to revel in my
Own worth
No one would listen or
Care
You enhance my
Relationships
Bring success to my hands
Impart Your wisdom
To my logic
Overturn kingdoms to
Bring Your will for
Me to pass
You are my great
Defender

233

❧

There is pending settlement
For the lost
The LORD of Hosts
Does not recommend
The curse of death
Call on Him to
Represent you in this
Trial called life
He brings to it the
Blessing
He is a seeker of
Truth and justice
Who sees into your
Heart

❧

234

❧

My spirit is quickened
To respond to the
Magnificent
Compelling
Voice of my God

❧

Another spirit moves
Surreptitiously to entice
My mortal mind

❧

All bets are off
The outcome clear

❧

A spirit quickened by
God will prevail

❧

Barbara Kelly

235

❧

Known equations
Seem responsible for an
Educated outcome
Nowhere has man recorded
All the equations of God's
Plan with its expected
Outcome
The ways are without
Number
Custom-fitted to each
Individual
Custom-tailored my life
To fit the Master's
Plan

❧

236

❧

Colliding spirits
Let God arise to
Influence the hearts
Of a confused man

❧

When the dust settles
There is not a demon
Remaining to elevate
Itself against the
Knowledge of God

❧

237

Ever-increasing wisdom
Eradicate the lesser
Standard of this mortal
Mind
I'm throwing wide the
Gate
Come in
The ever-increasing
Speed of time
Demands I increase
Sensitivity to my Master
When the hounds of hell
Follow hard on my trail
They are blinded by
The Astounding Light
Surrounding me

He increases as I
Decrease

238

The banqueting table
Is richly appointed
With red
Holding court with
The LORD of Hosts at
The head
The angelic army is
On guard
Come
Drink from the Fountain
Flowing from the throne
Of God

Barbara Kelly

239

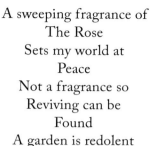

Rendezvous
Without restraint of
Time or space
A beautiful dance
In time with my
Heartbeat
Reminds me that a
Moment with You is
Greater than a thousand
Elsewhere
I know when mind
Body, or Spirit needs
Refreshing, I'll come to
Rendezvous with You

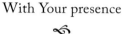

240

A sweeping fragrance of
The Rose
Sets my world at
Peace
Not a fragrance so
Reviving can be
Found
A garden is redolent
With Your presence

241

❧

Somnolent bones
The trumpet
Awakens to
Resemble the One
I knew
Walk with me
Into Glory

❧

Dance before the
King
Gather around
You those gone
Before

❧

Raise up dead in
Christ
We are in
Forever

❧

242

❧

Pressing onward
Into a realm of
Glory
Absorbing the Light
Pulling out all the
Gifts and desires of
My heart

❧

My Father treats me

❧

Barbara Kelly

243

❧

I give you Wisdom of
The ages
Take up your bed and
Walk out of these
Present circumstances
Blow the trumpet in
Zion
Walk, run to the Light
Never look back

❧

244

❧

Where does the
Anger stop
Can we anger and
Not sin
Righteous anger
Delivers a message
Of deliverance and
Motivation to rise
To higher heights

❧

Woe unto the ones
Who use Your name
To spew venom on
The Righteous in
Christ

❧

245

❧

Insufficient funds is not in
Your vocabulary
Scholars from around
the world
Debate with human
knowledge
With the Wisdom of God
There is not a dictionary big
Enough to contain Your
Thoughts of good, not
Evil
Insufficient funds is not
In Your vocabulary

❧

246

❧

The Flame stirred
Burns brightly
To reveal
Layers and depths of
Truth
Spoken with meekness
Bringing Peace
With greater
Understanding

❧

Barbara Kelly

247

⤬

Victorious Soldier
I am not moved by
What I see
My faith is in You
LORD of Hosts

⤬

The center of my
Eye is focused on
Things not understood
By mortal man

⤬

248

⤬

I have embarked on a
Journey
Fed and clothed in
Righteousness
LORD
Lift my eyes to the
Heavens
That I might see
Truly
Not jaded by things of
This earth

⤬

I will not twist in the
Wind of controversy
My sails are set
I am at rest

⤬

❧

I'm shedding these
Garments
Taking a bath in the
Oil of Gladness
Filling up on
Good Wine in new
Wineskins
Now dressed in Royal
Robes
I walk in the ways of the
Righteous dominion
Over all the kingdoms of
Darkness

❧

❧

Where there is Light
No darkness remains
Fill me to overflowing
With the Light of God so
All see and know the
Spectacular victory in
Knowing You as
Redeemer

❧

All of my household will
Now walk in the ways
The Light has
Chosen
They will not fall to
The left or right
Only trod the perfect
Center of the lighted
Path

❧

Barbara Kelly

251

❧

Wishing wells and
Fountains
Stone paths
Beautiful gardens
In glorious color
Benches set for
Comfort while I
Take in the
Bountiful Presence of
God
He reminds me that
This is a gentle touch of
Him
Heaven awaits with so
Much more

❧

252

❧

My spirit is a
Windswept plain
Void of all human
Habitation
Free from
Sand dunes
Watered by the
Fountain of
Life

❧

Satan has offered a
Palatable solution
I only hear the Voice
Of God
I choose life

❧

❧

As I transit the water
The lighthouse casts a
Strong and steady beam
I will not go under or
Be tossed
I set sail toward the
Lighthouse

❧

❧

The assembly of the
Darkest kingdoms with
Giant kings
Tremble in the wake of
My voice
Speaking in the authority of
My Father
The King of Kings
They run toward the
Places of their
Authority while I
Walk in heavenly
Places always
Mindful of The
Righteous King I
Am through Him

❧

255

᪐

Evil plots are being
Designed to interrupt
My destiny
Father says my end
Will be better than
My beginning
If I don't give up on
Him
He has not given up on
Me
His plans are to prosper
Me
Not to punish me
I cling to Him in this
Distress

᪐

256

᪐

A Witness-Bearing
Spirit
Looks at all my
Activities
To accept or reject
My behavior
According to how
I bear witness of
You

᪐

You never condemn me
In chastisement
Only reprove me in
Your own gentle way

᪐

257

⤢

Your soul is refreshed and
Your mind renewed
Your promises reach the
Heavens
To give way for rejoicing
In holiness

⤢

Release the balm as a
Solace to the nations

⤢

258

⤢

A winsome delight
Cracks the shell of
My heart
Causing Love to
Overshadow
All my doubts and
Discouragements

⤢

Oh Holy One of
Israel
Remove me to the
Place of Redemption
Where my heart
Remains true and
Full of Joy
Everlasting

⤢

Barbara Kelly

259

∾

Whether I leap or
Crawl
Walk or run
You are there for the
Journey

∾

You make my crooked
Paths straight and
Keep my feet from
Stumbling

∾

Your right hand is
My reward
As the crucifixion of man
Tries to say I owe
A debt I do not owe

∾

260

∾

I stood by the well
Watching as the Water
Filled my bucket
No more to thirst
I drank my fill
Satisfaction was
Always there for
The taking
Thank You for
Showing me this
Well that will
Never run dry
Where longings are
Met
Desires of my heart
Fulfilled and no
More night without
Illumination

∾

261

❧

The fatted calf is slain and
Cooked over the fire
Served with fresh Milk
Sweet Wine from the
Winepress

❧

There is dancing in the
Streets
While my Father beams
With delight over the
One returned from
The grasp of Satan

❧

The alleluia of
Angels resounds in
Heaven
I'm sure He is keeping
Score of the
Enemy's attempts to
Kill, steal, and destroy
There is Victory in
The camp

❧

262

❧

The Anointed One and His
Anointing have come upon
Me to speak the Word of
The LORD
The LORD of hosts in His
Name
He girds my loins with Truth

❧

How will You go forth
Do You see the futility of a
Servant who forgets His
Adoption into the Royal
Household
Hear the voice of the LORD
He prepared a Way
He opened the window of
Heaven
Oh You of little faith yet
He says I the LORD am
Your God never
I say never will I forget
my promise to You
Never
I watch over My Word to
Perform it
There is abundance for the
Taking
Come
Drink at this Fountain and
Quench the thirst or need

❧

Barbara Kelly

263

∽

A knot hole
An imperfect world
Hold me to the Truth
Satisfy my mouth with the
Good things You provide
Not what seems good in
The eyes of man
Forgive my stubborn
Excuses for not tasting
The Good Of The Land
Take away the cup of
Bile
Let the Son shine on
Your child

∽

264

∽

Hope in Glory
Let the Wind blow
Let the Waters abate
Bring Joy to my soul
I lift the Lamp to
Light the way
Bring me to Your
Dwelling place

∽

265

❧

The Law of the LORD
Is just and holds
No threat or guilt
It brings forth Joy in
The camp

❧

Surprise me, oh LORD
With that new thing
Every morning

❧

Come into this place
Let me see Your face
I need to see Your face

❧

266

❧

Satisfaction guaranteed
Quality is not a question
When Perfection Reigns

❧

Perfection became my
Redemption

❧

He gave it all that I
Might reign with Him in
Grace and Royal distinction
On the earth and in
Heaven

❧

Barbara Kelly

267

∽

Severely limited yet
I can do all things through
Christ who strengthens me

∽

My mind is ever renewed
By Your Word
It is brought captive to
Bow to Jesus in obedience

∽

Should I recall all the ways
And times of encounters
With the Holy Spirit
I would run out of breath

∽

268

∽

An affair of the heart
Not broken by
The untamed love
The heart of God
Ministers peace and
A tangible sense of
Acceptance and
Well-being

∽

Oh that the world and
Its confusion about
So-called love
Could reform its
View to know the
Splendor of You

∽

269

❦

Is the fire too hot
The snow too cold
Is ice forming on
The mind of my
Soul

❦

Don't forget to
Breathe the fresh
Undefiled air of
His breath
Breathe the nutrition of
His presence
Let it be, dear LORD
Let it be

❦

270

❦

If ever I assume
You are near
Counsel me with the
Wisdom of focus
Not a moment do I
Desire to move in
Any realm but Yours

❦

Overtake my harried
Self with Goodness and
Mercy lest I linger
In this fog of my
Own making

❦

Barbara Kelly

271

∾

To sever the spirit from
The soul
An act of Love
Leaving a whitewashed
Eternal assurance

∾

Nothing will supersede
This surgery
It is complete

∾

Drink deeply of the
Wine

∾

Heaven rejoices
I die to self

∾

So much more
Do I require
Only You
Only Your view
Completes me

∾

272

∾

Consciously I ask
Reveal a better way
To achieve the fortune
You have for me
Sweep me off my
Feet
Stand me on the Mount of
Olives
Tempt me not

∾

273

∽

My creation is
Struggling to
Break these
Bonds of
Humanness
To fly

∽

Take me where my
Flesh cannot go

∽

Uphold me with Your
Holy right hand

∽

274

∽

Are you sure of the
Stance you have taken
Is there Peace in the
Turmoil you feel
Can the Giver of Life
Equate with this unsatisfied
Thirst
Where is the voice of
Reason
Did I miss the bus

∽

Barbara Kelly

275

❧

Continue to eliminate
The dross
Have a heart
Take me into Your
Confidence
Lover of my soul
I crave You
Be my example of
Compassion with
Wisdom
Hold my being under
Your wings
No plague
No arrows
I watch the reward of
The wicked
My household is
Redeemed by
The Rock of my
Existence

❧

276

❧

Why not
No answer comes to
Mind
Evaluate the test
See if my life will
Sustain the belief

❧

You are God

❧

Pulsate in this mortal
Body

❧

Create the spirit
Of truth in me
As I shun the
Ever-present
Lies that try to
Confront the
Equality of my
Spiritual knowledge

❧

277

❧

I abide by the law of
Reciprocity
My claim to fame is
A walk with You which
Interrupts the
Fashionable trend to
Bow to Baal

❧

Broken fetters fall
All around me while
My God prevails and
His enemies in
My life are scattered

❧

Do not leave me
Unattended
The lusts of the flesh
Are about to overtake

❧

Come quickly

❧

278

❧

I relinquish this
Homeopathic process

❧

I leave my poor efforts
To clean up my act

❧

Nothing has prepared me
For this current

❧

Living does not mean
Life

❧

Where are You

❧

Do not see with my
Eyes the demise
Only with Your vision
Love me

❧

279

෴

No tears flow
Though my heart is
Breaking

෴

To know failure in
This venture
Gives no repose

෴

Come
Guide
Let Wisdom have
Her perfect way

෴

280

෴

The sweltering hole
I carve for myself
Has no air

෴

Bring Water
Load me with Meat and
Lots of Wine
Carry the Meat with Oil of
Rare vintage from the
Mountain of Olivet

෴

281

❧

I awoke to see the
Entrance of a thief
He thought to scare
Taking all
Withdrawing with a
Pack of lies on His
Back

❧

I wielded the Sword
Spoke the Name
Applied the Blood

❧

Let the Peace Passing
All Understanding
Wash me
Guard my heart and
My mind

❧

I saw the thief for
Who He was
He could not remain

❧

282

❧

A listening device hears
The utterance of Your
Spirit

❧

No technology is
Required

❧

Just lean into the
Realm of Heaven

❧

Listen
The trumpet is about
To blow

❧

Barbara Kelly

283

❧

Where superstition rests
There is a composition
Of fear and longing for
A sure thing

❧

I am established in the
Place of Honor
The Lord of Hosts is
My All

❧

He loves away my fear
My longing is to be with
Him continually
For eternity

❧

284

❧

There is a Seed of
Righteousness
Burgeoning in your womb
To be delivered forth this week
You will be set free to continue
The journey God has placed
You on
Forever singing a Song Of
Freedom to those who
Pass by
Embrace this Spirit Child
Who will grow to fulfillment
Within the year
No evil will fell this tree
With its sturdy trunk
Its branches will house
The needy
Who will harmonize
In
The Song
Of
Freedom

❧

285

❧

I swam the channel
Naked for the world to see
He clothed me

❧

My tongue spewed
Bitterness
He brought Honey from
The honeycomb
To feed me

❧

I chose to choose unwisely
He liberally gave me Wisdom
From The Throne of God

❧

When my faith wavered and
I was in despair
He gave me His Joy
Teaching me how to believe

❧

I will not follow the voice of
A stranger
Only
The voice of the LORD

❧

286

❧

From somewhere in the
Universe
There is a scream for
Liberty

❧

From outside my
Universe
Calls the voice of
Freedom
His name is
The LORD of Hosts
Jehovah Jirah
El Elyon

❧

Forever
I Am

❧

Barbara Kelly

287

❧

Your voice has merit
With God
He has emboldened
You to challenge the
Hearts of men
When they cannot
Will not hear
Your words penetrate

❧

Come to the celebration of
Heaven over you and
The many who have
A heavenly home
Because
You cared when
God called

❧

288

❧

A severance of my
Past supreme
Self-awareness
Leaves my anatomy
Whole

❧

Wherever the appendage
Hinders recovery
I choose spiritual
Surgery

❧

Love covers all

❧

289

❧

Thankfulness is an acquired
Habit
Reasoning is fruitless
Unless it's with God

❧

Come to the Fountain of
Truth
Drink until there is
No thirst
Bathe in the Brook that
Runs still

❧

For the excellence of
This Way does not leave
You thirsty or in
Want

❧

290

❧

Leverage upends my
Supposed importance
There is an unnatural
Force tipping the scales
To give me the edge

❧

No longer does Satan
Come out as a heavyweight
With all the building blocks
To kill, steal, and destroy

❧

I Am
Is the winner

❧

291

❧

A switch in my
Perspective
Has a profound
Move of The Spirit
In my life of
Boredom

❧

Living on purpose
Makes peace
Available

❧

A resemblance to
Peace
Comes in waves of
Uncertainty

❧

A Life in Christ is
Continually preserved
For all eternity

❧

292

❧

In between the
Lines is read a
History
Not paralleled
By current
Circumstances
Coals of kindness
Turn a heart to God
Teacher, teach me to
Embrace Life and
Blessings

❧

293

❧

A friend in these times
Is necessary for the
Orderliness of mind
The mind will trap
Death and curses to
Feed on
Never accept less than
Life and Blessings
Huge, huge Blessings
I forget not

❧

294

❧

My rainbow has a guazy
Appearance
The pot of gold is too far
To reach
The star I'm supposed to
Wish on has slipped out of
View
I've twitched my nose
Clicked my heels
Nothing

❧

I lay my heart bare
For You, and You reign
In me in Peace
You sing over me
I hear Your voice
A more plain Truth cannot
Be had

❧

Barbara Kelly

295

❦

Centurion
Guardian of my heart
From ancient times
Before the world began

❦

You looked upon me with
Favor
Have led me through the
Valley of the shadow
of death and
Brought me into the Light of
Your Lovely Presence

❦

I reverence You
I love You

❦

296

❦

I celebrate You
Lifting You up with
My praise
Exalting You above all
Other gods

❦

The angels come to
Feed me manna and
Fend off the
Hellish creatures who
Bring death

❦

297

❧

You have watched the
Move to undo all you
Have done

❧

Now watch the
Universe bow to
The Creator
Who ever lives to
Keep you in His
Promise
To elevate you
Before men
In order to see
His name reverenced and
Your name cleared

❧

298

❧

Let there be Peace to all
Who see me
Touch me
Hear my voice
He has searched for one
Who is blameless toward
Him and
Found me
With His outstretched
Wings
He covers me
Listening to Him leaves
Me speechless
Hearing Him brings to
Life the knowledge
Within

❧

Barbara Kelly

299

࿐

I waver not
People have no effect on
My spirit
Youth is renewed
Without the accompanying
Naivety
When God has His way with
My mind and heart
He speaks to people and
Places where no man can go

࿐

Yielded to You is
Assurance that Psalm 91
Is in effect
This is the true meaning of
Purity
Not my purity but
Yours

࿐

300

࿐

Joyous Savior
Flood me with the
Undeniable strength
From the Glory of God

࿐

To worship You is my
Highest goal

࿐

Entertain me please
As I entertain You

࿐

301

Bittersweet memories
Escape now and then
Wash them in Your Blood
Leave only the sweet part

Unholy ground becomes
Holy when You and I
Set our feet there

Unveil the darkness
So my feet don't stumble

302

From dimensions unknown
Drifts a cloud laden
With all things good
Have Your way
Don't delay
I'm waiting to hear
Your voice

When I tremble in the
Headiness of this
Occurrence
You come to me with
Peace
I surrender

Barbara Kelly

303

≪♭

Situate
Relocate
Underline
Underwrite
Measure by measure
Line upon line
Divine interference
Utmost Power
Driven Purpose
Steady Peace
Overcoming Joy
Lively precept
A way out
Time banished
Untold Grace
Boundless Mercy
Prospered by Your hand
No sorrow
No shame
Righteousness with authority
Your kingdom come
Your will be done
In me
As it is in Heaven
All this and more is
Mine
The ultimate conquest of
Your affection
Fulfill me to capacity

≪♭

304

≪♭

Major weapons of
Warfare are at my
Disposal
Undisclosed to the
Enemy
His camp is overturned
The Revelation is in me
To walk with God
Hear His voice
Hearken to His command
He is my Beloved
I am His
My covering is Love
Blood is the verifying
Truth of my heritage

≪♭

305

❧

My certificate of birth in
Heaven is forever settled
Bring me back home where
I belong
My heart's cry is to be with
My father for all time
I need You
Security of propitiation
Keeps me
Hold me
Forever in Your Loving
Care

❧

306

❧

Should I but take a pen
To write of You, there
would be no beginning
No end
A vast undertaking to describe
The Ultimate
All-Knowing God
Who was and always will be
The God
Who rescued me

❧

Barbara Kelly

307

❧

God Power
Man power
My choice
I choose God
Who sweeps over me
With His understanding of
My intimate thoughts
Gives me knowledge for
What I don't know
Hinders the word of the
Enemy
Becomes my Strength
When I'm weary
Shows me Beauty in
All things big and small
Is always glad to
Hear from me
Talks to me
Giving me insight from His
Heart
Oh, powerful God
Show me the ways of
Righteousness

❧

308

❧

Where is the water
Still but not stagnant
The meadow green
Without pestilence
I need to lay there and
Drink till I'm full
Hold my hand
I think I'm lost
Find me in this
Wilderness
Lead me on to the
Cup running over
On
My table of plenty
Always My Shield
My Strength
Falling is not an
Option
I am kept
Chased after by
Goodness and
Mercy

❧

309

❧

Whatever You do
You do so well that nothing is
Left to chance
You are full of power to
Overcome every other
Supposed god of man's
Making

❧

Wherever You show Your
Hand, I'm aware of
Changed circumstances
Rules rearranged
Hope deferred returns
No amount of persuasion
Can convince me of
Another power so pure
So sweet to my
Heart's need

❧

310

❧

A whimper in the darkness
Cowering from
The Light
Swerves at His rays
Screaming to be
Released into the
Bodies of man

❧

No human can fight off
The relentless
Attacks of hell's regions

❧

Thank You that
The redeemed say so and
The rescuer hears
We are not harmed

❧

311

❧

No answer is good enough to
Soothe my troubled soul

❧

Search me
Know me and all my ways
As I open the door for
Your Spirit to operate in
My life

❧

There is a thunderous roll of
Hell as it realizes my
Life is redeemed
Rescued and forever
Rearranged for Your
Pleasure

❧

312

❧

A double mind
Will not benefit
God or man
My focus will not
Be disturbed
Nor does the wind
Blow two directions
Without causing
Destruction

❧

313

❧

This is Your day of deliverance
From the evil ramification of
The evil one

❧

Rise and shine for
Your light has come

❧

The winter wheat has
Shown His head
The cycle is laid
Down
Refresh yourself by the
River Hebron
Drink deeply
Settle yourself before
The King
He is deliverance
Wrapped in Love

❧

314

❧

My Shepherd has spoken
My name
I do not want

❧

I see Your hand at work
Bringing me to the open
Door that leads to
Lush green pastures

❧

Will You take me there
Even now
I'm so tired of human
Endeavors to placate
This longing
More of You always
Less of me

❧

315

❧

The Judge has given the
Verdict
The judgment has been
Expunged

❧

My new life has no vestige of
Its former self

❧

Freedom is more than a
Release from bondage
It is the ability to walk in
Love, Power, and a Sound
Mind

❧

316

❧

A Metaphor
An Allegory
A Holy Grail
To drink from

❧

To find yourself
With Holy
Emphasis on
The way you
Walk before
The King
How you bow
To worship in
Allegory not a
Metaphor
Walk clean
See clearly
Have the time of
Your life

❧

317

∽

Living well
Is my Father's plan
No amount of dreams
Can outdo His desire
For me

∽

He has a hand in all I
Do
He steers my life out of
Danger and into Light
Because He Loves this
Errant child
Why would I choose
Another

∽

318

∽

I'm learning not to live in
Regret, rather to accept my
Father's quick and sure
Forgiveness
Moving on
I receive many blessings
Favor pushes aside any
Shame or fear
There is no time to look
Back
On a path with sure footing
Because of Jesus
My focus is on the
Mountaintop

∽

Barbara Kelly

319

❦

I stand in need of a
Savior
To You I give all brazen
Thoughts
Outlandish ideas
Longing without hope
Your Truth remains
Comforter of my soul
Sweet companion
Speak to my ravaged
Heart
Compel me with Your
Selfless Love
Guaranteed to sweep me
Off my feet

❦

320

❦

Whether I stand alone or
In a crowd
My Companion speaks sweetly
In my ear
His attention never wavers
My heartbeat is regulated by
His intense care ever
Present
No other Love can
Compare or is so
Colorful
What is the world
Without Him
And
His love

❦

321

～

Today will be my past
Tomorrow
So I'll walk in tune with
A different beat
Settle in repose while
My King sets the stage
For my next adventure
I can hardly wait
To walk into this
Incomparable
Life with Him

～

322

～

Sweeten my life with the
Real thing, no substitute
Bathe me in the Oil of
Gladness
Turn my waters into
Wine
Have Your way
With me
I salute You!

～

Barbara Kelly

323

⚜

Same day service
Washed clean
Pressed into His service
Without regard for
Color
Paid in advance
The life in Christ is
Forever
No claim check needed
My name is in the
Book of Life

⚜

324

⚜

Have You ever
Heard the song speak
God's presence
Removes all trace of
Human incompetence
The waves
Mesmerize
The sun set in regal
Beauty in the ocean
Surfaces or
Rises out of the east
With magnificence
How does a mountain
Evoke such a burst of
Hope and Love

⚜

325

≪

I wish for these:
A Wealth of Spirit
A Brilliance of Wisdom
Always a Living Epistle
A Natural Generosity
Superseded by His Spiritual
Abundance

≪

326

≪

A spring is welling up
In me
Fed by my Savior
I will fly with wings of
Eagles
My youth is renewed
My mouth has a
Satisfaction prepared
For this day of my
Life
I put Your Kingdom
First and
You delight in providing
All my needs and even
The desires of my heart

≪

Barbara Kelly

327

~§

A ride through my
Paradise is forever
Etched in my mind
Thoughtless adventures
Come to an abrupt end
I see my own reflection
In the pool of life
There is no glimmer
In the eyes
The partial abortion of
My peace is a sickening
Revelation
Return me to the spot
Where my goodness comes
From God
Where He talks and I
Listen, knowing my
Steps are ordered by
Him

~§

328

~§

My lamp is burning as
I carry it to light the
Way
Come
My Bridegroom
Meets me on this lovely
Path
Strokes my hair
Shows me the true
Meaning of romance
Whispering in my ear
The wonderful things
He has planned since
Before the time
Began
I'll be true to You
All the days of my
Life

~§

329

❧

Whether I hide, run,
Sit, stand, walk, talk, or
Remain silent
You continue this
Fathomless pursuit of
Me
No one has ever Loved
Me so
You Reign Supreme
Yet
You discern my most
Intimate thoughts
I love You

❧

330

❧

Hold fast to your
First love
He will impart wisdom
To deal with this new
Way

❧

His desire for you
Comes about daily
Whether your eyes
Behold it or not

❧

Look up
See your redemption
Fear not
You are sheltered
Under His wings
In His perfect care
Because He Loves you
His Word is forever
Working in you and
For you
Listen quietly
Hear the Voice of the
Ages tell you of things
To come

❧

Barbara Kelly

331

❧

I transmit to you
Through your pen
There is a dark
Horse riding among
You
Be prepared to do
Battle
Not in your own strength.
This is not a time to
Worry or fret
Just take up the sword of
Salvation
The battle is Mine
Says the LORD
This time between now and
Christmas will reveal My
Plan for your life
Keep steady
Focus
My arm is not shortened
Nor my face turne
Away from My people

❧

332

❧

A gala event is
Scheduled for you
Be prepared in your
Finest raiment to
Stand as My representative
Before dignitaries and
Kings
Loosen your belt
Don the robe of
Righteousness
Get ready
Your time has come

❧

∾

A random selection from
Among My people will
Rise like cream to the top
No promotion but Mine is
Necessary
A velvet tongue and
Back of steel are all that is
Needed
With Sword in hand
These will lead, execute, and
Deliver
Selah

∾

∾

The times
Are changing
The Set Times remain
Drink from the cup that
Never runs dry
Uphold victory
Don't allow any but
God's goodness to
Prevail
The footprints of time
Have already been laid
Walk in them
Circumspectly

∾

335

❧

Red, white, and blue
Blood, purity, and hope
Run with it
Never assume anything
All My will has been
Established
Be rooted and grounded
In it
See what needs to be
Accomplished
Do it
I will bring Honor and
Glory on your head as
A witness of my
Goodness toward you

❧

336

❧

A random tandem
With chalice in hand
Seeks praise and
Will walk as though
The Word is in them
No
And again
No
Do not be fooled
Man's way is not God's
Do not be overtaken
By despair
Let Me take all your
Burdens
You take My yoke
Upon you and be
In Peace

❧

337

❧

The proverbial brick wall
Jesus walked through it
So will you
All that is needed
I have provided
All your desires I
Desire to meet
Don't try to cross the
Bridge alone
Lean heavily on Me
Walk with Me
Talk with Me
I Mm
Your own

❧

338

❧

Have I ever told you
I would be there and
Wasn't
Have I ever promised
Wisdom for the occasion and
Not delivered
Isn't there always a way out
Do not stumble at My words
I will uphold you with My
Mighty right hand
I give you favor all the time
Take it
My disposition toward you is
Consistent
I have a banner over you
Proclaiming to all Heaven and
The regions of hell that
I love you perfectly
All of your days

❧

Barbara Kelly

339

∾

Somewhere in the midst of
All this chaos
Rises the Phoenix from
Among the ashes
Look to the east
Let the sun shine on this
Face
Live to Love by My standards
Hold dear all I have
Promised and told you
I would bring to pass
I Am and
I have a rich reward
Bless the Lord, oh
My soul, and
All that is in me
Bless His Holy Name
Forgetting not any of
His benefits
Pause and calmly think on
That

∾

340

∾

The willow is bent to
The ground
Boughs are not yet
Broken
The winnowing floor is
Swept clean
Everyone goes His own
Way to pursue the Bread and
Wine in their private place
Sweeter grapes come in the
Fourth season
No one wants to serve Wine
From bitter grapes
To sit under the willow is
Impossible
Seek a stronger bough to
Find repose

∾

341

The rope is for binding and
Hanging
It is also used for rescue
The sweltering sun can kill or
Warm the aching in my bones

I lift my eyes to the hills from
Which comes my strength
My Savior walks
among them to
Show me His Infinite
Wisdom
To talk without fear or
Bondage

Freedom is internal
Even if the fetters remain

342

I dreamed my walk with
God had been impaired
So I sat in His presence
To recover the relational
Experience
I cannot love otherwise
My ultimate purpose is
Elevated when I esteem
Him with my whole being
No other way is possible
My whole household
Serves The LORD

Barbara Kelly

343

❧

Let me be a sweet fragrance
In Your nostrils
Let the taste in my mouth
Be sweeter than honey

❧

When I lie down or
When I wake
Be uppermost in my mind

❧

Uphold me with Your
Mighty right hand

❧

There is so much to do
Spirit of God, move me
Into Your realm
Away from the
Maddening crowd

❧

My countenance is
Transformed by
Your residing Spirit
They are drawn to You

❧

344

❧

Wavering in this present
Crisis
Is not an option

❧

Stabilization is the
Key
To the higher call

❧

My spirit knows
Right well
Creator
Create in me

❧

Alive, well, prospered
I function in the
Meadow of Peace with
The cup Abundance

❧

345

❦

I hear the harp
The trumpet calls
My flame burns bright
LORD and Savior
Complete the work of
Royalty from Heaven in
This place

❦

Eliminate the working of
Many in darkness
Uphold The Word of
God in our government

❦

Secure our borders
Unleash Your wrath on
Demonic work in
High places

❦

Unravel the tangle of
Chaos

❦

Swing low, sweet
Chariot of God

❦

346

❦

Somewhere in the
Midst of all I know
Comes Triumph

❦

He rides through my
Heart with a sword of
Light

❦

My mind in
Acquiescence is made
Alive with Divine
Revelation

❦

Wherever You are
I find Truth

❦

Barbara Kelly

347

❧

The dry gulch is
Flooded
The trees grow
Flowers bloom

❧

My time has come

❧

To
Dance in the street
In joyous abandon
Singing in the
Voice of hallelujah

❧

No danger lurks
That holds a threat
I am sheltered
I Am
Protects me

❧

348

❧

Swimming upstream
The rocks break my bones
My arms cannot take the
Strain
Suddenly
The Force under my arms
Holds me
The stream switches
Directions
The floor is smooth
Showing me the better
Way
Where no stress is
Involved
Awake my mind from
This lethargy
Show me The Heart Of
You

❧

349

❧

These appendages
Do not belong
Sever them
I will not bleed

❧

Switch these thoughts to
Pure
No more suffering
Open the windows of
Heaven to
Reveal those blessings too
Big for my mind to
Conceive

❧

Holiness overtake
Somehow in spite of
My unique
Views
And those of my
Peers

❧

350

❧

There's a banner
Waving
Up ahead
I know it is the bearer of
Good News
So
I'll trim my lamps
Watching over the flame
There's a trumpet blowing
Stirring in my soul
Says the next thing I
See is
A single rider on a
Beautiful horse

❧

This is no joke
My time is here

❧

Barbara Kelly

351

❧

Where there's Faith
Answers are on the way
My needs are clear
Guide me into all
Truth
Settle the score with
Satan
His debt is mammoth

❧

There are light beams
Going up to Heaven and
Back

❧

God's word is True
Never fails when I
Ask
In faith
Believing

❧

352

❧

Why is this passion
Unanswered
Why is this rhythm
Not stilled
Can I remain here
Only to be denied
Fulfillment

❧

Create a new way
In me to worship
You in Spirit and in
Truth

❧

Nothing compares to
You

❧

353

✍

Save me from the
Homilies
My only inspiration is
From Your Spirit
Don't judge from my
Appearance
How the music starts
Or
How the dance begins
There is so much
More

✍

354

✍

Stir the waters
Let me see
Cross over the
Jordan
To freedom
My Egypt is in
The mind

✍

No tremor is under
Foot
The Everlasting is
Steadying my walk

✍

Barbara Kelly

355

❧

Thy waters overflow the banks
There is a balm in Gilead
Summer comes more
Quickly when
Winter fails
Bringing pestilence

❧

Regard the winter with
Spring on its heels

❧

A reminder of the New
Creation
The Hope of Ages

❧

Prolong the time of
Harvest

❧

Give us, LORD
A Few Good Men

❧

356

❧

The battering ram
Has withstood the test of time
Now is the time to open the
Gate
Let it swing wide
The battering ram was
Seized upon to belittle
The Hope born of God
I
Reached higher
Yelled louder
Settled the score
The winner takes all

❧

357

The withering vine
Tells of winter to come
A living cell beneath the
Soil promises a future
Renewed, refreshed, revived
Restored
For all time to come
Sweet Forever beckons
To the seed
Return the fullness of
The Promise

358

The reeds are blowing
In the wind
A sumptuous meal
Is set
The posturing of the
Swampland is to tear
Down the everlasting
Promise
I will not be moved

Barbara Kelly

359

❧

The river runs
The clouds are
Dark
The hills are
Alive
The rocks cry out
This is The Day of The
LORD.

❧

360

❧

Redeemer of Life
Snatch us away
From death
Hold us to Your breast
Send forth angels to
Bring all that
You have promised

❧

361

꘡

A circle within a circle
A wheel within a wheel
The all-seeing eye
Searching the
Soul of man
To cleanse and
For freedom to rise
From the core

꘡

362

꘡

Surrender in the crosshairs of a
Cannon bears no
Resemblance to
The voluntary
Hanging on a tree

꘡

My surrender came as no great
Price to me—just knowing
The Great Shepherd says
I do not want

꘡

Wherever temptation
Arises
My heart cries to You
LORD
There is no want

꘡

Barbara Kelly

363

✺

Rewind
Complete the call to
Stand
Offer incense to Heaven
See the worthless offerings
Without meaning to a just
God
Call to the heavens with a
Glad heart
Rejoice in this current
Wilderness
Knowing
The road is leading you
To a prosperous end
Without a sorrow or
Persecution
He has already overcome

✺

364

✺

Suspended between then and
Tomorrow
I dare not look down
The net has been removed
He is undergirding me
There is a Lamp on my feet
His Spirit is a Light
On my path
I will not fear but
Focus on the eternity
Embodied
In Him

✺

365

❧

Swifter than the stream
Flowing around my ankles is
The beating of my heart
His will is perfect and pure
Allowing my heart to soar
With wings
To talk with Him face-to-face
To know with His assurance
I will not fail
I will not bend or bow
I will be all He has called me
To be in Him

❧

366

❧

I expect what You say
Will come to pass
The source of my belief is
Written in Your book
Implanted in my heart
Spoken to my spirit
Holy Lamb of God
slain before
The foundations of the world
I believe

❧

Barbara Kelly

367

❧

Playful, tempting
Offers are accepted
Blindly without thought for
Tomorrow
The dark horse comes
Riderless into our
Midst
Speaking volumes
Concerning
Your Overcoming
Power and Grace

❧

368

❧

Listen to the
Tumbleweeds roll
The mockingbirds sing
The mountains offer
Magnificence
I will rejoice in the
LORD
He gives me His strength
My voice is raised in
The wilderness
To capture The
Hope of the nations

❧

369

કે

Overlay the stench with
Perfume
The stench will remain
Cover the flaws with
Beauty
The work is never done
Hold kangaroo court
The law has not been
Upheld
When will they see and
Know
They need Jesus

કે

370

Beloved Assurance
Come quickly to this
Battleground
Heaving earth is
Yearning for You
Hold back our enemy from
Destruction of our land

કે

Barbara Kelly

371

❧

The grave has been opened
The one who goes there
Is not concerned with
Political procedure
Only with
Heavenly Grace and
Restoration to The
Creator of The Created
One

❧

372

❧

The swing vote
Says okay to a volume
Too loud
Listen in the quietness of
Dark to a voice with
Resonating sound of
True Freedom

❧

373

❧

Wherever I walk
You are there
I have Your authority
Your name is on my tongue
There is ownership where
My foot sets
Remind me to thank You
With my lips and
Lifted hands
You are Grand

❧

374

❧

Not now
My heart screams
Not now
My mind pleads
My mouth says
Thy Kingdom come
Thy Will be done in
Me as it is in Heaven

❧

Barbara Kelly

375

❧

The darkened glass
Keeps me from seeing
Clearly
The object of my
Affection and His perfect
Plan
Wait
Some of the fog is
Lifting
The sight is from a
Deeper place than my
Eyes
The kingdom is from
My Creator
I see more clearly
Through His eyes
My heart soars with
His Love
The Love that supersedes
All other

❧

376

❧

Subliminal messages are
Before me
My spirit receives only
The voice of my God
Written in the wind is a
Fleeting wave of false hope
No stronger arm than that of
My God
Upholding me
Awakening me from a
Place of reticence to
See the unknown
Future more alive than
The blood in my veins

❧

377

❧

I'm lifting my eyes to
The hills
My thoughts on
The everlasting
Do not require
Penance
Only focus
Father, speak
I will listen

❧

378

❧

Leisure is only
Appreciated if You are
Involved
Creativeness cannot be
Valued totally unless
You are the acknowledged
Creator
Beauty is in the eyes of
The beholder when that is
You
You see only beauty in
Me
My love for You
Astonishes me

Barbara Kelly

379

❧

Decades have passed
Since first we met
The road has been very
Rocky
You were always the
Rescuer of my
Stumbling feet
You always brought
Comfort and Peace
I love You
Everlasting One
Without You
I do not exist

❧

380

❧

Lover of my soul
Whisper to this hungry
Spirit
Talk to me about Your
Heart's desire
Allow me to have this
Relationship without
Restraints
Something is not
Registering
Please
Make clear Your Heart

❧

381

❧

Where do You
Sit down
Where is Your
Throne
Can You see me
Do You hide Your
Face in the midst of
My distress
You said
You would never leave
Me
Please
Reveal Yourself

❧

382

❧

The drum is rolling
For
The entrance of a
New name
The stage is set
Costumes not needed
Be yourself
Come as You are
The facades are lifted
No more night
Only Light

❧

Barbara Kelly

383

❧

Consequences demand a
New attitude
No promises of the
Impossible
A return to You in
Control of this
Place we call home

❧

384

❧

Before my eyes the
Drowning is taking
Place
Without a whimper
The Lamb is led to
Slaughter
Daughter of Jerusalem
Come forth
Sing the Song of
Victory
Walking with the deceived
Let the reward of
The wicked
Be in Your hands
I am the seeker of
Truth

❧

385

❦

The Door only swings
One way
You must go through
Not
Around
This trip through the
Door is a one-time
Thing
Thankfully
None of my foolishness
Changes the journey
On which I have
Embarked

❦

I walk with
Confidence in
The One in whom I
Have believed

❦

386

❦

Searching through the
Darkness of my mind
I cannot see the Truth
My spirit is battling my
Mind for supremacy
Somewhere I've learned
The Truth waits in
The shadows of my
Mind to welcome
Me with open arms
Into His beautiful
Presence

❦

387

❧

The how-to book
Forgot to mention
The dance between
Spirit and mind
Come home
The hour is late
Whispers the Lover of
My soul
To prosper and be in
Health is my quest
I will continue to
Dance with The Spirit
Leading
Oh
Holy One of Israel

❧

388

❧

Clarity please
No obscurity
Blessings flow to
The need
Desires met
Wisdom prevail
Let
Freedom ring
God's way
Not mine

❧

389

❧

Weep no more in the
Waterless cistern
Dry the feet of the
Washing
Settle the dust of
Camels
Wandering in the
Desert
A blossom is seeking
To bloom there
A cremation of former
Things
Without remorse for
What was never meant
To be

❧

390

❧

I sit in The House of
The LORD
Where I am
He is
No scorn is present
In the place of Love
Bringing the Good News
To a confused and
Dying world
The summation of
Kings and kingdoms is
In my knowledge of
Him
The Anointed One and
His Anointing

❧

Barbara Kelly

391

✌

Division of the pure
Of heart from
Influence of Satan
Is fathomless
There is no joining of
Forces between
Light and
Dark
Choose today
Whom You will serve
Don't wait
Time is in the now
Repent
Believe

✌

392

✌

Something ungodly is
Settling itself up in
Your life
The enemy has blinded
You to The Truth
Speak to the author of
Confusion
Tear down the strongholds
Walk free
See The Light
Bask in Peace

✌

393

❧

Wherever there is a
Radical need
My LORD abides
Offering a balm to
Heal the broken state of
Wholeness

❧

The palm is waving to
Separate the
Foreign emissaries of
Hell

❧

Atonement by Blood
Releases all from
Bondage into
Glorious Light

❧

394

❧

Summer is gone
A whisper in the trees
Says
Autumn would reveal
The far-reaching
Outcome of these
Current decisions
When winter arrives
The trumpet will call
The banqueting table is
Spread

❧

Barbara Kelly

395

❧

Illiterate and
Cast down
No one knows He
Exists but
Jesus

❧

The roll is called
The hopelessness is
Replaced with a
Robe of righteousness
Without spot or wrinkle
There were stains
No cleaners could
Remove

❧

A miracle took place
Woe is the one
Not willing to accept
The change

❧

Call for pity from
God
Who is not willing that any
Should perish

❧

396

❧

There is an oath
Sworn in Heaven
Concerning my destiny
That oath will survive
These wicked times
It cannot be broken
Except by me
I will not
Disturb the covenant
Made in Heaven
Executed by the
Holy Spirit
I exalt the God of
My salvation

397

The arrested quality of
The beliefs of some
Leaves those around them
Uncertain of
The Supreme Divine
Nature of Your Holiness
Unable to change in
Your views or take
Back Your Word
Thankfully
I am not moved by
These who underestimate
You

398

I have arrived at a
Conclusion
My life only matters
In You
No one has authority
In what I do or who
I am
But
You
When tempted to feel
Despair
It's the belief that others
Shake my confidence or
Fulfill my destiny
No one can
But
You

Barbara Kelly

399

❧

The seeker of Truth is
Rewarded
With a clear vision
A steady walk

❧

New information from
The Throne of God
Washed in the
Stream of Living Water

❧

Restored to righteousness
By
The Name Above All Names

❧

400

❧

There is no law but
Mine
To obey

❧

By obeying My law
You will be
Honorable to all other
Laws of the earth

❧

My ways always
Supersede
Human understanding

❧

The earth will
Rejoice in the end
For
The obedience of
My Sheep

❧

401

✍

Where there is
Truth
I Am

✍

I overflow in situations
Allowing Me in.

✍

Truth
Is My calling card

✍

Let Me show You the
Overflow

✍

402

✍

Savoring The
Wine
With an outburst of
My Spirit to
Settle the issue of
Financial freedom

✍

Barbara Kelly

403

∽

The hart is
Jumping
His hooves are
Laying hold of The Rock

∽

The mountain is
Bowing to
His Presence

∽

The Eagle is at the
Top of
The mountain

∽

Spreading His
Wings
Over
Jerusalem

∽

404

∽

The good of all
My footprints are

∽

From The Blood

∽

I've walked through

∽

Criticize
Agonize

∽

But
Realize

∽

No Name
No Blood
No Sacrifice
But
You
Cleanses me from all
Unrighteousness
Sets me upon
The Rock
Telling me of the
Assurance
I have
In You

∽

405

❧

He weeps in the garden
No more
But
Sits at the Right Hand of
The Father
Ever making
Intercession for us
Who are in Him
He administers His
Health and prosperity
Into us

❧

He is regimenting the
Armies of angels
Sending them to
Gather round
His children to
Help us get ready
For the honing of
Our destinies as we
Anxiously await
The trumpet sounding
To
Call us Home

❧

406

❧

Sweeter than my
Finest hour
Is the meeting
Preset
With
The King in His
Throne Room

❧

Reservations were
Made in 1943 with
No thought of time

❧

Seasons have come
And gone
The Time Is Now
My robe is ready

❧

I'll switch off the
Light before I go
Please come along
I know You will
Enjoy the party

❧

For Eternity

❧

407

❧

Swerving to miss the
Curveball
I fell into a pit

❧

He lifts me out of the
Pit of destruction

❧

While setting my feet on
Holy Ground

❧

He Lights the Way
Teaching me to
Catch the ball and be
Rewarded by
Him
In His
Righteousness and
Abundance

❧

408

❧

The deed to the
Inheritance has been
Given
The door of the vault
Swings open to reveal
The many Treasures
Within

❧

Life sustained
Becomes rich
The future known
By
My Father

❧

It is His Joy to
Tell me the Grand
And
Glorious
Plan for my life

❧

As I open my
Heart and spirit
Please
Reveal

❧

409

❦

Aligning my will with
His
Produces power to
Overcome the
Enemy

❦

Washing by His blood
Works miracles in
Mind
Body and
Spirit

❦

Oil and water mix
Bringing about
His will by
His Spirit
In me

❦

Now
I say

❦

Bless The LORD, oh
My soul

❦

Let God arise and
His enemies be
Scattered as they
Behold
His banner
Over me

410

❦

Let the Finder of God

❦

Touch the unknown parts

❦

To heal, seal with Life
And
Deliver from the
Grinding lie of the
Devil

❦

Look up
Open Your mouth
And
Let the God of Light

❦

Flow into Your
Mouth and filter
Through Your body's
Organs

❦

You will hear a lilt in
Your voice
Never heard before

❦

Those around You will
Be arrested by Your
Voice and demeanor
Reflected by
His Light
His Glory is manifest

❦

Barbara Kelly

411

❧

Maybe I'll live

❧

Closer to The Truth

❧

Maybe I'll walk
Only
In The Light

❧

Maybe I'll
Surprise hell
With
The presence of
Glory on my
Face
No darkness can
Hide

❧

Maybe others will
Benefit from
My proximity

❧

412

❧

Crawl into the
Dust at my feet
You peril from hell

❧

I grind You down and
Give no place to Your
Efforts

❧

I Am
Above and not beneath

❧

You do not have my
Mind, body, or
Spirit

❧

Without a doubt
I will hear only
The voice of
The LORD

❧

413

❦

Somber
Without Joy

❦

A dullness of eyes

❦

Bespeaks a
Heart
Without

❦

The Joy Of the LORD

❦

A cumbersome walk
Is
Not the walk of a
True believer

❦

Freedom from the
Bondage of familiar
Spirits

❦

Leaves me to fly
With wings as
Eagles

❦

414

❦

Deliberately moving
Into You
I ask You to breathe
Breath of Life
Over me
Allow me to know
The Truth in all
Matters
With angels in the
Watchtowers of my
Life
Look on me with
Your unfailing Love

❦

Barbara Kelly

415

꙳

Without crime or
Prejudice
No interference
From satanic lies

꙳

I will see You high
And lifted up
Without a flaw

꙳

Others will bow to
The name of Jesus

꙳

The mountains will
Fall

꙳

The waves will cease
To roar

꙳

The moon will not
Shine in the night
For
There will be no
Night

꙳

416

꙳

A voice crying in
The wilderness was
Answered

꙳

Temptation in the
Garden was
Repealed

꙳

Death by crucifixion
Brought Life

꙳

Eternity rests in the
Hands of The Mighty
God
Who will return to
Take me home

꙳

417

❧

It is more than wealth and
Riches we crave and know
You give
It is now a walk on
Holy Ground
With You
How precious is this time
With You
All the time
In the now time

❧

Dance with the angels
Sing A New Song with
The choir of the
Redeemed

❧

Willfully choose to
Grasp the
Blessings of God
In order to be a
Blessing

❧

418

❧

Let the rain fall
Let the wind blow

❧

I will drink to my fill
And
Be
Justified
By
Majesty riding on
The wind
With rain in my face
I'll visit
The Throne
Of God and
Speak in heavenly
Terms

❧

Barbara Kelly

419

❧

The well runs deep and
Clear
Do not drink there
Sediment collects in the
Bottom

❧

Swift running water is
Safe to drink

❧

The Watchtower sees all
Around You
He is a Hightower
Do not fear

❧

Dance in the moonbeams
Sing to The God of Your
Choice

❧

Prove Him now
See that He is able
To do more than You
Can ask

❧

He will teach You
To receive

❧

420

❧

Stay to the side of a
Landslide
At the top
You'll go down
At the bottom
You'll be covered up

❧

Stay to the side of the
Landslide
With God's
Perspective on the
Quality of the
Silt

❧

Listen to the cry of the
Seagull
What does He say
Concerning Your
Future

❧

421

᠀

A noose is loosely hung
About the man's neck
The stool he stands
on is broad
Tall and sturdy

᠀

He could release his neck or
Refuse to see this salvation

᠀

We all watch
Without a word of
Condemnation
Or
Redemption

᠀

Who is at fault that he is
Still standing on the
Platform of his own
Making with a rope
Hung loosely about his
Neck

᠀

422

᠀

Where will I be in
the midst of
This kingdom

᠀

My table is set
My lamp is burning

᠀

To allow the Bridegroom
A path of light to my
Heart

᠀

I'm lifting the veil
He is full of wonderful
Delight
At the view of me

᠀

I welcome Him with
Humility and The Fullness of
Grace into my chamber

᠀

Barbara Kelly

423

❧

The tree was hewn
Birds even ceased their singing
Joy came in the morning

❧

Dawn is on the horizon
Once again Joy comes in
The morning

❧

Hope is surging to the
Top of my consciousness

❧

No blame, no judgment
No anger or offence
Is compatible with the
Righteous white robes
I wear

❧

To let flesh depart and
Only Spirit remain
Is my heartfelt desire

❧

424

❧

These that You have given
Me
Are precious to You and
Me
My feet have trod here
It belongs to me
In order that they
May belong to You

❧

Sever all that does
Not belong to You
Let right standing
Prevail in the
House of The Living
God

❧

425

❧

Great oracles have been
Written, sung, and
Forgotten

❧

Do You remember the
Hushed tones of reverence
The unabashed songs of
Glorious exhilaration
The worshipful stance

❧

Do You consider the
Ways of man in light of
Your Glory or in the
Presence of Your
Mercy and Grace

❧

426

❧

Singularly my hope
Is fixed on Your
Beautiful face

❧

The presence of life
Situations
Drifts to the faraway
Background
When I remain
Steadfast in my
Gaze

❧

You look at me and
I see all I have need
Of met in Your
Loving eyes

❧

Hopelessness is met
By Hope

❧

Barbara Kelly

427

❧

Serenity of purpose
Calmness in the midst
Of
Chaos

❧

Is a reflection of You

❧

Creator
Create in me the wholeness
Where I digest
Manna
Considering Your care
For Your children

❧

428

❧

Honey from the Honeycomb
Is dripping into my
Mouth

❧

Nectar from the
Exotic flower refreshes

❧

Moonbeams filter into the
Night to remind me of
You
Sunshine is over my
Days

❧

I am blessed

❧

429

❧

Sincerity bounces off
Brick walls
When no Truth follows

❧

A whip is raised
No one is attentive
Thinking
What a beautiful man

❧

Listen to the
Reverberating sound of
Horses' hooves
Is he white
Is he flying from
The east
Do I hear a trumpet

❧

My lamp must remain
So I can see in the
Darkness and
Choose the right path

❧

430

❧

A wild array of
Choices
Makes decision
Harder
Change must come in
The form of Holy Spirit
Leading
Do not be fooled
God is not mocked
Change has become the
Key word when no
Definitive word would
Commit the speaker to
Ultimate good

❧

Barbara Kelly

431

❧

How do I compare
The compromise to
The Promise

❧

Will the Dove cry for
Lost humanity

❧

Do the times
Indicate demise or
Are You only
Watching the ebb and
Flow of humanism
For answers to this
Dilemma

❧

432

❧

Swinging on a vine
Grapes fall down
Someone must crush
The grapes to bring
Forth Sweet Wine

❧

Somewhere a Ram is
Caught in the thicket

❧

He is sacrificial for
Atonement
When blinded eyes
Cannot see the cross

❧

Watch out for
Artificial sacrifices
Without sufficient
Help in time of
Need

❧

433

❧

The land of Goshen is
Your home
Leave the unsettling
Place and walk with
Your head held high

❧

My people who are
Called by My name
Will change to meet
My standard of living

❧

I do not change
So
You *must* change to
Meet my standards

❧

My way is Kingdom
Way
No want is here
Step up

❧

Change is in the
Very air you breathe
Not from the
World system
But
From Me
Almighty is My right
Hand to the deliverance
Of my people
Shalom

❧

434

❧

Eat, drink, and be merry
Your Light has come
You are held in a
Very, very Strong Tower

❧

Weep no more for
The untoward ways of
The pagans in high places

❧

The lamentations of the
Saints have fallen on the
Ears of a Just God

❧

His Will is to bring all
Into the kingdom of
Righteousness

❧

No more will the cedars
In Lebanon bear the
Heavy-laden branches or
Shelter the wayward

❧

Call out to the God of the
Universe and be blessed
By His merry heart
Toward You

❧

Barbara Kelly

435

❦

Splitting hairs leaves a very
Slender thread
From which to swing over a
Precipice

❦

Too many fallow grounds do
Not bring a good harvest

❦

Shelter is only found where
Many dogs lie

❦

Don't wish upon a star and
Expect an answer to your
Dilemma

❦

436

❦

Your fingernails are dirty
From digging in the
Soil with toil
While the treasure
Is in the topsoil

❦

Crave only Me
With all your being
Look up and see
Your Redemption

❦

Clean your nails so
Others can see the
Overcoming Grace that
Cleanses you and delivers
You
Into that place of
Prosperity
Body
Mind and
Spirit

❦

437

❧

Somewhere lodged
in my mind
Is the mystery of who You
Are
My DNA was established in
The Garden of Eden

❧

How could it be that only Your
Spirit can lift the veil of this
Mystery and let me walk
Free of human constraints

❧

Shenandoah of the Weeping
Willows calls my name
Return me from the
Valley of shadows to
The sunshine of Your
Grace

❧

I remember You

❧

438

❧

Whippoorwills are calling
Listen
There is a message to those
Who understand the
Signals from on high

❧

Squandering the gift of
God is not recommended

❧

Even now
He is salvaging what and who
Belongs to Him
From the heaps of
Satan's destruction

❧

Nothing can ever separate
Us from His Love

❧

Not even the plans of
The evil one
Squelching man's
Devotion to Him

❧

Barbara Kelly

439

～

Is there a listening heart
Hear what I have to say
You are welcome in My
Presence
Welcome in My home
I surround you with
Volumes of Love
While stampeding the
Unwanted one and his
Works
Goodness and Mercy follow
Yes
Even catch up to you
To allow you free
Passage into My
Presence
Come

～

440

～

Clever ways
Destroy higher plans
Be my shield
Cross me over Jordan
I will sing of Your
Mighty Right Hand
Keeping me
Shepherd
Lay me down in those
Green pastures
While still waters beckon
You lead me not into
Temptation
You deliver me from
Evil
Jerusalem is calling me
Home

～

❧

Leverage
Intense leverage
Is being levied
To tax my soul

❧

Heavenly ramparts
Redeem me
Oh what Joy Divine
I am untouchable

❧

❧

Is the appropriate time
Now
Do the linguistic experts
Agree that
We are all speaking the
Same language

❧

It's a language of the heart
With a loud cry
To the universe to
Respond to its needs

❧

I've crumpled the
Paper
Turned out the lights
Still
I hear the cry of many
Hearts
Just like mine
Seeking answers that
Resolve
Tampered
Logic

❧

Barbara Kelly

443

Withholding is not
Conclusive to Peace

Waterfalls when paused
Are
No longer waterfalls

While listening to the
Overwhelming
Self-righteousness of
Wrong
The stilled voice does
Not make it right

444

Switching my allegiance
Causes me to miss the
Call of
Eagles
To soar through the heavens
I won't be traveling
Through space and time

With
Anyone else but
You

445

❧

Surrender the
Situation
Without complaint
Settle all argument with
A fine tooth comb
Giving no reply until
Freedom of Spirit
Flows through your
Mouth

❧

Do not bleed from the
Heart that has been
Mended by Supernatural
Force

❧

Concrete Evidence says
You are the overcomer
Through Divine connections

❧

Screech to a halt in all
Your finest efforts to
Listen
While your heart seeps
Blood
Get on track
Back to the future

❧

446

❧

The probability law
Creaks under the weight of
Assumption

❧

Wherever the road less
Traveled leads is sure
To offer newness of
Mind and heart

Cross the road as
Necessary to get a
Different view
Ponder all those
Things with an ear
To God and His
Point of view

❧

Barbara Kelly

447

❧

Repeat Your plans in Me
Repeat them until
My spirit resounds
With You and heavenly
Sounds

❧

Undo the tangled mess
My wounded self
Repeats

❧

Overpower with Your
Boundless Love, Mercy
And
Grace

❧

448

❧

A grove of lilies
A tree trimmed with
Dollar bills
Swinging on a star
Witnessing a conversation
With the kingdoms of
This earth
Do not seem so strange
When I gaze into Your
Lovely face and
Comprehend with
Humility how truly
Unfathomable and
Awesome are Your
Works

❧

449

⤫

While sitting in this
Place of honor
My impulse is to feel
Unnatural and
Unproductive

⤫

Remind me of Your
Plan
How it's never
Unprofitable to listen
To and walk with
You

⤫

Allow me this moment
To take it all in

⤫

450

⤫

There's a hole in your
Sweater
Mend it before it completely
Unravels

⤫

There's a crack in your
Cistern
Mend it
Or it won't hold the
Water that feeds you

⤫

Swelter in the Son
And purge yourself of
Poisonous toxins

⤫

Leave behind
Unwanted treasures
They will haunt you

⤫

Believe
Above all else
You are strong and
Capable
To run this race
With Grace

⤫

Summarizing
Live with the
Expectation of
Eternal Glory and
Earthly Power in Christ

⤫

Barbara Kelly

451

❧

Whether I sit or stand
My mind stays the same

❧

I no longer have a desire
To think these thoughts but
They continue
In a rhythm with the
World of confusion and
Unholy desires

❧

Redeemer
Unleash the blessing and
Make me wholly able to
Receive
On the narrow path

❧

I purposefully yield to
You and Your prospective
On what is for my best
Interest

❧

452

❧

Notoriety
Slams the door in my
Face
No new slant comes
Do you want to place a
Bet on the outcome of
This stifled attempt to
Follow after my Spirit
And not my flesh

❧

Nothing outweighs the
Plan of God designed just
For me

❧

453

❦

Sweeten the pot
With a new
Day of revelation
Without blinders

❦

Never has the
Request been more
Sincere

❦

Have a heart
Hear my plea

❦

No more biding
Time
Extend Yourself
To the exercise of
Teaching me to
Excel

❦

454

❦

Cream of the crop
Without a blemish

❦

Only the pure of heart
Solicit Your campaign
For righteousness

❦

We stand while
Others fall
Because our home
Is secure in The
Kingdom
Not a hair can be
Lost or shoelace
Counted as gain
From an unlikely
Source

❦

Without a snare I
Yield to The Holy
One and His
Anointing

❦

Barbara Kelly

455

Somnolence is the
Result of
Satan's attempt to
Strangle the resources of
The Holy One to rescue
Mankind from his
Insufficiencies:
Sin, Sickness, Death

Resolute in my desire to
Follow Holy footsteps
While always alluding to
The other side of the
Coin

456

Tricks of the trade
Do not hide Your face
I need to dine on the
Wine and Oil and
Unleavened bread

Wholeness of mind
Is my guest
Show me the
Healing Surge of
Power

457

❧

Quixotic
Along the edge of
Mount of Olives
Is the reminder of
The One who
Rescued me

❧

Enemies of my people
Want the rights to
The Honor God has
Placed there

❧

458

❧

Never more sweet is
This time when my
Agendas fall to the
Ground

❧

The elevation of Spirit is
Truly tonic to my
Soul

❧

Allow me to see the
Pumping of the blood
In Your veins

❧

Purge me with this blood of
Royal origins

❧

Presence of Your Spirit
Guide me into
All truth

❧

459

❧

The cane brake
Eliminates candor of
Soul and spirit

❧

The wailing of those
Who paid the price
For freedom of
Truth
Cannot get through
Without my
Underlying pain
I would not live to
See the Glory of
The LORD

❧

Bring me closer to
These trembling
Lips of the past
Seeking a listening
Ear

❧

460

❧

Savoring the Joy of
Your presence
I look to the day
When gazing into Your
Face will be so
Sweet and yield only
The Peace of Heaven

❧

Lately I seem
Distracted from
My true calling

❧

Sweep over my
Distraught mind
Beleaguered by
Earth's darkness

❧

Some of the Light
Has began to dawn

❧

461

✧

When the seer sees
The knower knows
The outlook holds
Abundance of
All that is good

✧

Miraculous is
My Father's house
Where the
Outlook is only
Good and glorious
With plenteous
Abundance to
Those who
Believe

✧

462

✧

Groundless motives
Come about as surely as
Curses coming causeless

✧

Little foxes have eaten
Away at the root of The
Vine

✧

Remember the days of
Noah
Pray to establish the
Pure relationship that
Calls unto Deep

✧

None can rely on
Relentless gossips that
Insist on the
Honor of being your
Friends

✧

Pass them by in favor of
The only Abiding
Friend
Who causes you to
Triumph

✧

Barbara Kelly

463

∽

Will you relinquish
Control of finances
To meet *all* your
Needs

∽

Will you put the
Net down to bring
Untold harvest

∽

Will you
Who know
Sit by
While opportunity
Passes

∽

Surrender now
To the
Lord of Hosts
Bringing forth
Gladness of heart
Knowing
He has heard your
Voice

∽

464

∽

My heart sings when
I remember
My Beloved's Voice as
He sings over me

∽

I exalt the One who
Knows me best and
Holds the world in the
Palm of His hand

∽

Do me the honor of
Receiving
The everlasting
Prize of Your
Presence to wash
My face that it
May shine in the
Brightness of
Your
Likeness

∽

465

∽

Clever is the hint of the
Unswerving sorcery
Pulling you to accept
The lie

∽

Should the evil one
Prevail
The God of Israel
Will rescue the dying
And care for
The perishing

∽

He has split the veil
To show us His
Marvelous Mercy
Goodness and the
Absolute defeat of
The dark side of
Life

∽

The Light now shines
Into the corners of
My heart
So that the darkness
Is overcome

∽

466

∽

I walk
Though You teach me
To fly

∽

I reminisce while You
Make memories of
Tomorrow

∽

Lean on me
You have said
While I struggle
To even stand

∽

Listen
You say
When deafness
Threatens

∽

Look long into
My face
Find comfort
There
While my eyes
Seem dim of
Sight

∽

Overtake me now
With the Overflowing
Cup of You at Your
Best with gladness of
Heart and the assurance of
Good to come

∽

Barbara Kelly

467

❧

Jesus got in the way
He is The Way
The Light has shown in the
Darkness
The darkness has flown

❧

Woe is the man who
Stands in the way of
Righteousness
Let Wisdom have Her
Perfect work

❧

The thorns of life have
Tried to destroy the
Garden of God
Remove them

❧

The Banner over you is
Love
Show no weakness
Let His Joy be your
Strength

❧

The hairs of your head
Are counted
None is lost

❧

468

❧

The Holy Spirit
The Rose of Sharon
The days of Wine and
Roses

❧

The Bride is ready
Lift the veil

❧

Hosanna to The King
Awaken the righteous
Sing the song of
Redemption

❧

Holy, Holy, Holy
Lord God Almighty

❧

Transfer The Goodness of
God into the hands of
The believing ones of
The kingdom

❧

Sweeter as the days go
By
Lighter is the load
When it comes from
God, not man

❧

469

❧

Hounds of Heaven
Arrayed for battle
Hell hath no fury
Like these from Heaven

❧

Batten down the hatches
For the wind will blow and
The earth will quake but
You will be held safely
In the arms of
The Good Shepherd

❧

God says,
Enough
It is My turn to
Overshadow the
Work of Satan and
Annihilate his
Big boys

❧

470

❧

Your home is my home
The candor of our
Relationship is unsurpassed

❧

Let's light the candles
Create a musical atmosphere
Drink the Wine
Sing a Song to the lover of
My soul

❧

Come home
My Lord
Beckons

❧

Barbara Kelly

❦

Israel, oh Israel
I have longed for you to
Take your rightful place
In the winner's circle
My heart pleads with you to
Call upon the Lord of Hosts
Jesus is His name

❦

I have not forgotten you
In this time of rebellion
The ones who say you are
Through do not recognize
My promises cannot be
Revoked

❦

Rise up, Daughters of Zion
Remember your loss of
Favor no more

❦

We have a destiny
Together
And none can stand
In the way

❦

❦

There is a fragment of time
To establish Your
will upon the
Earth

❦

I lift my eyes to The Hills
Strength comes

❦

Summer is on the horizon
Will winter follow

❦

When the sparrow falls
King of Kings sees
Therein is the solid
Hope that assures me

❦

Singer of Songs
Sing over me

❦

473

❧

Where will it all end
Circumference or
Diagonal

❧

To the untold remains
Of Your plan
Sale of the centuries is
Happening

❧

Will You please remain
In the heart of Your
Remnant

❧

474

❧

I surrender to The
Lover of my soul

❧

My new heart is in love
With You

❧

Somewhere in the history of
Me
Makes reality say
Your Love looks beyond my
Irritating sinful ways
To this reborn
Spirit's delight

❧

475

❧

The stranger calls stop
The voice I hear is The
Voice of The LORD
A stranger I do not
Follow

❧

Jehshua
My I AM

❧

I am
Set free
Redeemed from the pit
Healed
Made righteous by Him
Set in a large place
Covered with The Blood
Made in His Likeness
Whole in body,
mind, and spirit
Lifted high above the
rabbling crowd
Given The Desires of My Heart
Loved by
My Beloved

❧

476

❧

The line is drawn
Locution may change
The meaning is clear
My crown and robe are
Righteous through Christ
Jesus
Those who walk on the line
Soon fall to the other
Side
Where darkness prevails
My authority says no
To the executioner

❧

477

❦

Your covering is so
Complete
My eyes cannot see
My ears cannot hear
What You have in store
For me

❦

You come with such a
Sweet fragrance
Let it rub off on me

❦

Your Light is so bright
May others witness the
Glow in me

❦

You are Love and Mercy
These have kept me
I will extend the
same to others

❦

478

❦

You are a behemoth
Blocking my view
You resemble the
Mountain I have
Already called down

❦

Get out of my way
In Jesus name
And
By the way
Don't come back

❦

479

❧

Wilderness is not
My home
Awaken to The Call
Seize hold of the
Promise

❧

The land I go to is
Full of plenty
Flowing with Goodness
Grace and Wisdom of
God

❧

There is no gap
Between Thee and me

❧

480

❧

The face of complacency
Is worn by those in
Power on this earth

❧

He who reigns on high
Will overcome my world
Set the record straight
Show me The Ways Of
The Lord

❧

No more inconsistency
When Heaven reigns in
The midst of terror

❧

481

❧

Sunday is coming
I'm circling the block
Do I go into the
Traffic of life
Split the roof
With force
To see the sky
Without blinders
To recognize the
Promise spoken in
My ear
I am in authority
Here
To destroy the works of
The devil

❧

482

❧

Little do I know the
Ways of God

❧

My intellect goes
Haywire when the
Eyes of my inner
Self are open to God's
Call and Plan

❧

Where are those footsteps
I am to walk in

❧

Show me Mercy
Lift me from this
Insurrection

❧

While I wait upon You
I will Sing A New Song

❧

Live as though The
End from the Beginning
Accomplishes
His work in me

❧

483

❧

Whither Thou goest
Lead me
Whither Thou lodgest
Bring me

❧

The hallelujahs
Ring through Heaven at
My compliance

❧

Willingly
I am
Drawn

❧

484

❧

Contrary to popular
Opinion

❧

Sticking your finger
In this dam
That is about to break
Loose
Is
Not only
Wantonly ineffective
But deadly

❧

Open your eyes to the
Master of
The deep

❧

Let go of this
Obsession and
Become
Victorious

❧

485

❧

The barn door is open
The cattle have escaped
But not far

❧

Look to The Hills
Draw your strength

❧

These hills are full of
Gold and Silver

❧

The Eagle is flying low

❧

Recognize The Voice of
Jehovah

❧

Create a place for Him to
Dwell

❧

486

❧

Savior of my soul
Divine Nature
Dwell in me
My end is hope filled

❧

Where to access
Your Greatness
How to display
Your Love

❧

Barbara Kelly

487

❧

The tide has turned
Washing the shore with
More force

❧

The circle is complete

❧

Watch
Wait

❧

Secure your heart
To The Heart of The
Almighty

❧

Spring
Summer
Fall
Winter

❧

It is over
Reach up

❧

488

❧

Swinging from the rafters of
Indecency
Over a pit of fire

❧

You think your efforts to
Destroy Good
Are succeeding

❧

Never looking up to see the
Armies of Heaven poised to
Annihilate this course of
Destruction

❧

God's own will pull out in
Time to secure their position
In The House of The LORD

❧

The Eagle is not blinded or
His wings broken
He flies in majesty with
The ardor of Heaven and
Earth beneath Him

❧

489

❧

Creatures of the deep
Respond to the resonance of
The Sounds of Heaven

❧

None will be freed from
Bondage until He appears to
Redeem His own

❧

Trees clap their hands
A cry comes from the rocks

❧

The winter is over
Joy to The LORD
My Redeemer Lives

❧

490

❧

The waves lap against the
Shore

❧

Seagulls patrol

❧

The Deep cries for
Its creator

❧

Can you see with
Unclouded eyes

❧

The Eagle flies
Overhead

❧

There's a mountain
In my vision
It is The Hill of
Zion

❧

Barbara Kelly

491

❧

Effervescence on the
Surface

❧

Peel back this layer of
Confidence

❧

View the untold
Misery in this heart

❧

Somehow The Light
Must shine beyond the
Overeager smile
To see and show The
Truth

❧

To one so deceived
Self must surrender

❧

Hello
Good News
The Heavenly Peace
Awaits

❧

492

❧

Shining through this
Present darkness
Is a Truth so strong
It will cease chaos
Overturn the
Fowler's plan and
Streamline
Governments
Undo reckless
Behavior and
Bring Peace

❧

The Living
Shalom
Remains

❧

493

❧

The swindler
Has stolen the
Last batch of
My people

❧

I am sending a
Restoring
Lightning to flash
Through poisonous
Reflections of
Distortion

❧

To bring the
Ultimate Plan of
God to
Illuminate the
Earth and

❧

Bring His children
Home

❧

494

❧

Sweet is the savor of
The Meat I eat

❧

The simple milk
Sufficed at one time

❧

Now, Savior
I requested a fulfilling
Meal at the sumptuous
Table set before me
In the presence of
My enemies

❧

My cup runs over with
New Wine and
Fresh Oil
The Bread is
Broken
From Age to Age
I will praise to
The Staggering
Presence of
Jehovah

❧

Barbara Kelly

495

❧

Listless winds blow
And now are
Picking up

❧

Let the Rain fall
We are so thirsty
Bring strength to the
Weary
Release the Spirit of
Truth
Blow The Trumpet
Loud

❧

I succumb to
The Ruler of The
Universe and me

❧

496

❧

He is the Lifter of your
Head
He is your Shield and
Buckler

❧

The road is winding and
Long, but not arduous

❧

Sweeter is success when
You drink The Wine
Seeing the future through
God's eyes
Brings miraculous
Results

❧

Don't delay the process
Of
Surrender
It is not hopeless but
Full of the Goodness of
God

❧

Hold fast to your Redeemer
As He unveils precious
Gifts you have required
Of Him

❧

Be strengthened and
Encouraged
I Am with you
I will not forsake you
No, never

❧

497

❧

Cleansed lips and a
Pure heart are
Receptacles for The
Holy Ghost to pour
Into

❧

The richness of Him
Divides bone from
Marrow

❧

Without rancor
He willingly
Supplies
All you will
Ever need

❧

Lean not unto your
Own understanding
Let God be God

❧

498

❧

The mile marker
Suggests it's time
To exit

❧

However,
The Ruler Of My
Heart says
Tomorrow will come
Soon enough

❧

Listen
Watch
Keep the candle
Burning

❧

Barbara Kelly

499

❧

Hoe the row you've
Been given

❧

Sweep it clean
Begin again

❧

Sooner than you think
There will be a
Harvest beyond all you
Could ever think
In the light of
This world

❧

No one sees beyond what
God has allowed

❧

I allow a true vision
God is bound by His
Word to allow this
Also

❧

500

❧

I've broken through
God's Grace
Assaults my senses
I cannot do less than
Obey the call of
One who knows me best
Which way do I turn
Toward The Light

❧

501

❧

The waters have parted
Walk through on
Dry ground
Do not camp here
I will walk with You
Through this valley
Leave it all behind
Don't look back
Your enemies will be
Drowned
Completely washed
Away
Never fear
I Am with You
Always
Think on these things
Ponder the Goodness of God
In this time of tribulation

❧

502

❧

Your quiver is full
Father
We, Your many
Children
Seek to develop in
Your image
As You lift up the veil
In this final hour
We see the Glory Of
Your Grace
I savor this moment
In time while
My lamp is trimmed
Burning bright
Divine Harmony
Ushers in Your
Presence
Love of God
Overtake me

❧

503

God knows your heart
Has been broken
He is mending it, so it's
Better than new
It's restored and reaffirmed
By the Lover of your soul
He will Love you so much
That no man will ever break
Your heart again
He does not want you
To allow anyone to come
Between
You and His Love for you
Seek God's Kingdom and
His Righteousness
First, and He will add all these
Other things to you (as
what to wear, what to
eat, where to live, etc.)
Matt. 6: 33

504

Do You remember me
Just as You said I should
Remember You
Allow me to see the
Untold mystery
That holds my future
These mindless efforts
Are not the
Destiny
You said was in me
Spirit Led is my desire
Love Divine is my
Only quest
Arrange the schedule of
Heaven's desire for me
To be revealed
Thanks

505

❧

The apparent nuisance
Of the opponent is a
Mere unworthy
Appearance
An apparition of no
Consequence
When the enemy
Looks you in the eye
With so-called documents
Of doom
Do not wrestle with him
Let go and determine
To settle in your mind
That nothing shall by
Any means hurt you or
Cause you shame
There is no color like
White to denote
Purity
But this purity does not
Touch the Touch of
God's Greatness to
Overtake and overshadow
You
Let go
Let the Author and
Finisher of your
Salvation have control

❧

506

❧

Oblivious to the rabble
I'm moving in The
Spirit of God
In order to possess the land
There is no authority
Like the great God of
Israel to challenge
My insane thoughts
Bring Peace in the
midst of chaos
With no remembrance
In Heaven of my
Shortcomings—I'll
always bow my
Knee to The God of
My Salvation

❧

Barbara Kelly

507

❧

Woe is the man who walks
In darkness
While saying
Continually that He
Sees Light
Water erodes metal to
Rust
Pluck the cinders from
Your eyes
See with clarity
The rusty water You
Drink

❧

508

❧

Who is this Jesus of
Nazareth
Who is The One who says
He is coming soon
Once again
Worlds were formed
At His Word
Darkness snuffed out
By His Light
Who will defend me
Oh yes
The One whose Spirit
Fills my mouth with
Words like honey
To cut to the bone marrow
To reveal Truth
The magistrates have not
Heard
There is a cleansing of
Things prayed
No stone is left unturned
Revival awakens those
Dead bones

❧

509

❧

Severance is not enough
I've seen this reward for
Doing Your will
Likewise my cup
Overflows and pours
Over the sides of this
Table set before me in
The presence of my
Enemies
Let the wind blow
Igniting the Fire
Within me
Showing forth great
Things in healing of
My body and
Prosperity of my
Financial affairs

❧

510

❧

Buried deep in the
Stones of iniquity
There is an unbroken
Seal of Light
When these stones
Bump up against
Iniquity long enough
Light will shine through
For the opportunity
To take over the
Usurped life
The owner of these
Stones must not
Waver in his choices
But
Turn to The Light

❧

Barbara Kelly

511

✍

The Watchful Eye
Never sleeps or slumbers
He sees your pain and
Shows forth mercy
Renders the fowler helpless
Against the vengeance of
God
When the snow falls
The time will be
Ticking toward a
Heavenly move upon
The earth
Singular vision is
Necessary in this hour
Do not stray to the
Left or right
Walk circumspectly
Before The God of
The universe
Seeing Him as your
Father who Loves
You and is The one
Who redeems you
From the pit of
Destruction

✍

512

✍

Trophies won
Ribbons displayed
Pretorium of highest
Regard
Do not compare to the
Crown of Glory my Father
Bestows on my head
Oh what a wonderful thing
To know The Wisdom of
God
To have His Knowledge to
Guide me in this
Supernatural walk
You will exalt me in due
Time to the calling in
My life
Thank You

✍

513

❧

Cremate my flesh in
Order that my spirit
Born of You is in control
Use the leverage of
Heaven to move this
Mountain standing
Between us
How great and really
Stupendous is The
Grace in my life
Without overstating
I lift You above all
Other gods
Giving You all Glory
Honor and Praise
You are beautiful

❧

514

❧

The little I know
Leads me to believe
The Lover of my soul is
Saying
The best is yet to come
We walk not by sight but
By Your Spirit
The leaves are turning
It is time
The time is now
A year has passed
We walk closer to The Truth

❧

515

∽

Stretching my mind
Toward
Things unknown in this
World system
Seeing, listening
Always seeking
To catch a glimpse
Of You
Hear Your thoughts
See Your face
Listen to Your
Heartbeat
Thy will be done
Thy kingdom come
Lord Jesus

∽

516

∽

Remembrances
Bring thankfulness for
My ancestry
On earth
The teaching of You
The biblical connection
To Abraham, Issac, and Jacob
Holy is The Lord God
Almighty
Sitting at the right
Hand of my Father
Forever making
Intercession for me

∽

517

❧

Seeking to plumb
the depths of
Time
I was before time began
You say the plan was
Established
The payment made
All Heaven agrees
Whether I sit, stand, walk
Talk or remain silent
You are there, here
Everywhere
Why worry or fret
You said, "If You be for
Me
Who
Can be against me
Shoulder to shoulder
Jesus and me
To conquer the enemy's
Stance in the lives
Constantly contorted by
His twisted ways

❧

518

❧

Sharing your heart with God
Walking circumspectly with
Him
Knowing His Word as clearly
As Your own
You cannot fail
Let the axe fall
But not on you
You have been made for
Greater things than the
Games people play
They serve a different
Master
Do not bow to their pressure
Lift up your head to
The One who Loves you
Make Him the controller
Of your life
Easy does it

❧

519

❧

If I look left
If I look right
With my eyes open or
Shut
You overshadow me with
Your wings
There
I am safe
With You
You don't lie to me or
Deceive me with a glib
Tongue
Thanks for being exactly who
You say You are and that
You do what You say You
Will do

❧

520

❧

Where there is an
Attitude of Peace
A firm stance in the
Midst of war
A longer, wider view
Than the best projectors
You hold The Winning
Card
Trumping all other
Players
Will they ever be
Surprised

❧

521

From the looks of things
You hold the keys to the
Kingdom
Why hang your head
When Jesus is the lifter of
Your head
Why strategize
When He says He is your
Shepherd and
You do not want
If you really, really try
You still cannot add a mere
Inch to your height
Stand back
Here comes
The One
Who will never, no, never
Leave you

522

Are you heavily laden
Jesus said,
Take My yoke
My yoke is easy
My burden is Light
Rise up
He is The Lifter of your
Head
Step out knowing
He watches over your steps
Lest you are dashed against
A stone
Look upon His lovely face
Who shines in an unearthly
Light
He views you with utmost
Compassion
He will protect you with
His Shield and Buckler if
By His Spirit you are
Led

❧

The playing field is leveled
Sweet water flows
Through your body
Your eyes are bright
With the luster of
Divine Health
While the whore of
Babylon puts forth
Her last effort
You will be assured
You have won
Seek first The Kingdom
With all its righteousness
The winner's circle awaits
You
Go with the calm demeanor of
One who knows the call is
From God

❧

❧

These present circumstances
Defy logic
Remember Me
You said
I have delivered you
Healed you
Set you high upon the rock
I have renewed your youth
Satisfied your mouth with
Good Things
Appropriate for this time of
Your life
With my wings spread over
You
No evil shall befall you
No plague come near
Your dwelling
Hear My voice
Hearken not to a stranger
I give you Peace
My Peace
I give you
It's not over until it's over
My return is soon and
Sudden
Watch and wait

❧

525

❧

A windowless home
Absorbs Light
Open the windows of your
Soul
Let The Light come
pouring in
Savor the sweetness of My
Presence
Wherein there is Peace
So long as your eyes are
Staid upon Me
My Light will illuminate
Your path
Do not seek to know all
The future brings
Rather
Know what is
Truth for
Today
I will not let you down
Don't you see that all the
Voices bringing unrest and
Confusion are not
My voice
I love you with a Love
Everlasting that is
Uncompromised

❧

526

❧

From Everlasting to
Everlasting
I have known you
As you give place to
Me
I will impart words of
Knowledge and Wisdom
I will show you things
To come
I will strengthen you for
The journey
My angels have charge
Over you
They never cease doing
Their job
The windows of Heaven
Have opened
My Grace is sufficient for
You to walk in
With Godliness

❧

527

≪

No stranger shall enter these
Portals
The summation of your life
Is culminated in this time of
Waiting
Watching and surveying
How Good the Blessings
No stone will be left
Not turned
The true meaning of
Your life is in the
Telling of the tale of
The underside of
These stones
The brook ripples when a
Stone is thrown in but a
Boulder sinks to the
Bottom
Watch over your life to see
From the prospective of
God
No stranger shall enter
These portals
Says the God of the
Universe
Your Father

≪

528

≪

Seventy times seven
Appropriate
To dissolve the
Nasty behavior
But
Even more effective
To remove the
Timber from the
Forgiver's eye
No notion in the
Mortal mind can
Truly be blessed
Except by the Divine Nature
Stamping this
Mortal idea
With His own
Some subtle move
In the mind of
Limitations
Can remove all
Human limitations
Giving instead
Wings to fly

≪

529

❧

The Lover of my living
Lets all of Heaven
Loose to
Align with Him my
Humanness
Then I see with
Bold eyes
A new day dawning
With new purpose of
Heart
To melt away sorrow
Signal, Lord
When You finish with me or
I might just go on forever

❧

530

❧

Swimming before my eyes is a
Plethora of all the good things
God has in store for me
My eyes behold the
Glory of The
Lord
Without earthly conditions to
Overshadow my vision
You speak of more than my
Heart can contain
Thank You for Your
mindfulness
With gifts to show Your
Love

❧

531

❧

Simpler times cut into
Memories
Making one forget
The hard part
No time is left to
Those who wait
Yesterday begins
Tomorrow
The longest mile is really
Short when you truly
Belong to the One who
Makes your life complete
Rave reviews are given to
The God of your salvation
The One who knows your
Name

❧

532

❧

The encumbrances of your
Heart have been
Lifted by Father
To give you a journey
Without bowing down
No one can secure your
Load but Him
He lifts your head and
Sings to you what's on
His heart
Listen closely and be
Amazed at the anointing
His heart places on you
Sing Hosanna
Let the rafters ring
Alleluia to The King

❧

533

❧

If swimming upstream
Gives you satisfaction
Don't grieve when you
Have no time or energy to
Give
If swimming downstream
Brings boredom and a
Lack of thankfulness
Don't grieve when no
One understands
You
Look up and be blessed
The hills are alive and
Full of music
Reminders are all
Around
Open the blind eyes
Let the soul rejoice

❧

534

❧

See
Hear
Smell
Walk
Run
Live
Laugh
Love
Bless
Encourage
Draw away
Create
Dance
Sing
Rejoice

❧

Barbara Kelly

The sometimes Voice
Is actually the
Full-time Voice
The changing of the tide
Brings good and bad
Choose Good
Evil will always prevail
My allegiance is with the
One that brought me
Running to the High Tower
I find Comfort
No foe can interrupt

Shanghaied by the
Deserter of Heaven
Wallowing in a sea of
Remorse
Why do the present
Circumstances overcome
Your knowledge of God
Wonderful are the
Feet of those who
Bring Good News
Good News is in you
Live and let live
Without rancor
He will bring you
Into the valley and
Out again into The Light
Don't sway or faint
Just continue
On the path you have
Chosen

The pot of gold is
Simmering on the
Back burner
Look into the things
I have set before
You
Do not be intimidated
By naysayers
Cling to Me and those
I have put in your
Life to believe with
You
There is accomplishment
In what I have for
You while you
Keep Your perspective
Always defined by what
You believe to be True

I look into Your eyes and
Wonder of wonders
I see You looking at me
Looking at You
Thankful that what You
See is a reflection of
You in my eyes
There is no space or
Time in the way You see
From the time before
Time began
I was in Your eyes
Lift me to that place
You have planned
To be the You in me

539

≈

Without exception
You never fail
Failure is satan's
Design for man
I succeed
Because You are
Success
No, no, never will You
Ever leave or forsake
For You are
Incapable of ever
Going against who You are
Help me to never go
Against who You are

≈

540

While the lemon drop
Is somewhat sweet
The end result is
Bittersweet
Somehow the confusion
Exists saying to follow
The evil one brings
Pleasure without pain
The end result is
Bittersweet

≈

541

ॐ

The lingering sweetness of
Your Presence is
Sweeter than the
Honeycomb
More satisfaction than
The honey it holds
To eat of the meat of
Your Word
Fills to the full
Not leaving want
When the Wind of Your
Spirit
Refreshes
Soaring with Wings As
Eagles
Seems effortless

ॐ

542

ॐ

There is a pit prepared
For my enemy
I will not go there
The sprinkling of blood
Has prepared my heart
To repent
I live in the shadow of
The mercy seat
Sonshine is on my
Face
Listen to the sound of
Heaven
The trumpet calls

ॐ

Barbara Kelly

543

∾

Your day has come
Wake up
The lofty presence of
Your enemy has fallen through
The ground
Lift up your head to the
Maker of your Peace
Wrestle not against flesh and
Blood
It is fruitless
See beyond these present
Circumstances
There is a willow tree
In your yard
Dig it up and let the
Lilies grow
The wind is giving you a
Message
Pay attention

∾

544

∾

Believing is receiving
Stagger not at the Promises of
God
You are the called
Chosen because of
Your diligence
Before Me
Do the good of mind and
Purpose in your heart to
Follow blindly when I call
Knowing I will never let you
Fall
Fear not
You were created for My
Purpose
Designed to accomplish the
Wonders only I can
Bring to pass
The future in Me is secure
You do not want for any
Good thing
That comes from My Riches
In Glory

∾

545

There is no room in
My house for
Idols
It is swept clean
The Holy Spirit is the only
Apparition allowed
He alone holds the key to
My heart
His Love washes over me
I am complete

546

Clear the webs from your eyes
Contain the Goodness of God
Be willing to see
Others as God
Sees them
Do not allow the enemy to go
Unchecked
You are a receptacle of God's
Precious presence
With the Beauty and Grace He
Has bestowed on you
You will miss the greater
Gifts if you continue
To limit God
Yield to Him in complete
Sacrifice
Don't forget to condemn
Every high and lofty thing
Exalting itself against
The Knowledge Of God
Bringing everything
Captive to the
Obedience of Christ Jesus

Barbara Kelly

547

≈

In spite of what seems obvious
There is much, much
More for you to learn
Much more for Me
To teach you
Let your hair down and the
Chips fall where they may
People are not your answer
Listen for my instruction
Watch while I turn
Heaven and
Earth to do my bidding
Christians belong
To me and are
Your family but
Not all are mature enough or
Close enough to Me to have
Your best interest at heart
Awake to the New Day I have
Planned for you
With the abundance I Joy
In giving you

≈

548

≈

The sun rises
The moon sets
There is a tremendous
Mountain
Moving
That door is open
That door is closed
Move, move, move
Be fearless
When the mountain moves
You will see My sheep
Grazing in green pastures in
The valley below
What a treasure
Awaits you there
Hold fast
My dear child
To The Hand that never
Changes
Give a shout for Joy
Huge victory awaits

≈

∽

Without comparison
To any other
You will always stand complete
And entire
Wanting nothing
Similar circumstances will
Always prevail
The sure answer is Jesus
Summation is
You are complete in Him
All you need do is ask and
He will promptly search
Your soul for unfettered
Belief in all He is
Then all of Heaven and Earth
Yield to His call to answer
Your prayers of trust and
Belief
He will not fail in your
Behalf

∽

∽

Worshipping The King
Without a doubt
Without a whimper
Troublesome times
Awaken the need
Hope is restored
Lift the Banner High
The Banner is Love
Without spot or wrinkle
I stand
In awe of You
Christ, the Sovereign
King

∽

Barbara Kelly

551

❧

Harmonious and sanctified
Is the upright walk with Him
I was put in my
Mother's womb
With His Spirit in attendance
Quilting the pieces of my life
He knew my end from my
Beginning and was always
Ready to throw the warmth
Around me when life
Seemed too difficult
He is here now to inspire
My thoughts with the
Wonder of Himself

❧

552

❧

Taste and see
That He Is Good
The Liberator of
Mankind
All things are
Possible
He writes the very desires
He puts in my
Heart

❧

553

❧

Let me be a witness to
The unseen
Masterful plan
Guide me into all Truth
That my words will
Inspire others to know
You and Your Redeeming
Grace
With uncommon grandeur
You speak so that the most
Common man will know
Truth and behold You

❧

554

❧

Aggrandizing the
Human efforts
Springs from
Insecurity in God
The Father, Son, and The
Holy Spirit
When He is lifted
High above all man's efforts
He will Honor and Favor
and Glory in this
Child

❧

555

Somewhere in the midst of all
The chaos
I hear A Sweet Voice of
Godly reason and perfect
Understanding of my
Imperfection
How I love Thee
Sweet Repose
Uncompromising Mercy
Let me hear and know You

556

Circumcision removes
The unwanted
One day in solitary
Confinement
With You
Exceeds all the
Experts in chaos
Winging it is
Not from The Holy One
He presents a plan
To follow and
I am blessed

557

∽

You are the chosen
Not only called
Secure Your future in
The One who has set
You high upon The Rock of
Your Salvation
When your feet tire
He will carry you
Always close and
Ready with all His
Heavenly assets
Don't underrate Him
He will supply
Liberally
Withholding nothing
Walk on
Hang on and live

∽

558

∽

The wind is whispering a
Song
Coming from Mount Zion
Saying
Come to the mountain called
Calvary
Little do they know the
Urgency of that whisper
The water flows deeper and
Deeper
Sing hosanna to the
Almighty One
The King of The Jews

∽

Barbara Kelly

559

❧

A wish come true
A desire met
A window opened to
Release acute
Abundance
How can we understand
Except
By The Spirit
I will run the race with
Grace
Goodness and Mercy follow
Me
I'm on the way home

❧

560

❧

Whither Thou Goest
I will go
Whither Thou lodgest
I with pleasure
Will lodge
My people will be
Thy people
For they are taught of
The Spirit
When I arise
The dawn warms my
Face
When I retire
The star-studded sky is
My cover
I await the trumpet call
From my Lover
Holy, holy, holy
Is The Lamb
Slain from the
Foundations of the
World

❧

561

❧

The hoary head of winter
Has departed
Can you perceive the
Gentle breeze and
Singing of birds on the
Wing
You can sing the
Hallelujah chorus
Without shame
Throw out the coin, which
Will return with gladness
Step lightly
Sing loudly
The Spring is Bubbling Up
Through your veins
To herald the Awakening of
All That Is To Be

❧

562

❧

The Great Good News is
In you, Bob
To show the entrepreneurial
Enterprise of God's choice
Set your mind on Me
Do not be filled with
Other schemes, plans,
and adventures
I have put within you a
Plan to engage you in a
Challenging endeavor
Let Hope spring up in
Your innermost parts
I see your potential and
Passions
I happen to have
Put them there
Rejoice
It is A New Day

❧

Barbara Kelly

❧

Dearest Beloved Father
How do these lips of clay
Speak of the untold
Mysteries within
How do the angels
Contain the knowledge of
You
Without a doubt
My soul sings at the
Thought of you
Knowing I am Your
Child
Your girl
Your daughter
Wash me clean once
Again by Your Blood and
Your Water
Strife is my enemy
I ban it from my
Existence

❧

❧

The Winter of my soul is
Giving way to the
Everlasting Spring
Woe to the one who
Tramples on my journey's
Path
My God Reigns in The
Burnished Gold of my
Reborn Spirit
Lying down in Green
Pastures
Looking into Your
Beautiful Face
I'm In The Palm of Your Hand
Nothing shall by any
Means harm me
My table is set
Behold The
Bridegroom Cometh

❧

565

Driving out the
Useless bantering
I come
Without fear of rejection
The Holy One is on this
Child
Severing all past
I look to the exciting
Future You have
Planned
The future is Now
Abandoning all
That is not Your
Will and plan, I come

566

Harsh reality will
Banish Faith
Being in this world
and not of it
Allows my Faith to build
Acknowledging the
Encumbrances do not
Belong to The Believer In
Christ Jesus
The heavy weight has been
Lifted at the cross
Holy is The Lamb of God
Who is My Salvation and
The Lifter of My Head

Barbara Kelly

567

❧

Wishes do come true when
Based on God and His Word
Accruing unholy wealth is
Going to fail
Look and see that God is
Good
Never evil
Base all your predictions on
Him, His Word, His Blood
Contrary to your past
Is a huge Blessing
Having been promised
Long ago

❧

568

❧

I've swept away the
Cobwebs
I've built you a home
To your specs
All these Good Gifts are
In My hands
The Provision is never
Lacking
My Word says you will have
More than enough with plenty
To provide for others
I put in your path
Your husband is your
Head and I Am
His Head
All is well

❧

569

❧

Come on in
The water's fine
Come sup with Me
Give me your
Undivided attention
I want to tell you of
Things to come
As the world continues
To race ahead at a
Crazy pace
I have my plan in place
You have a place
Where the economy is
Good
Where Favor Abounds
When danger is at hand
It can't find you
Because you are
Sheltered under My
Wings
I give you Grace to
Walk through the
Lowest valley
I am always with you
Always

❧

570

❧

The syringe has
Removed all temptation to
Follow human instincts
Below the surface of
Tomorrow is a waft of
Sweet fragrance
Unknown to mortal man
Awake and see that God is
Good
No evil befalls you
No plague comes near
Your dwelling
Witness with your
God's eyes
The total redemption of
You
From the
Early demise
Satan has planned
Tomorrow is a new
Day
Tomorrow holds the
Divine Purpose of His Plan
He has not forgotten you

❧

Barbara Kelly

571

✍

The summation of all my
Days
Comes as no surprise
A visitation to the world
We know
Without citizenship
A King is my
Father
My life is in
Abundance
Due to my Father's
Provision

✍

572

✍

Nourishment from the
Bread of Life
The showbread is now
Served
I watch The Divine
Purpose for this
Pageantry
It seems my frailty is
Overcome by His
Watchful eye
No other can satisfy

✍

❧

In supping Wine
Comes
A Thorough Cleansing
Wholly accomplished
By Grace
By delight and utter
Confidence
The Giver of Life
Welcomes me without
Hesitation
Into The Holy of Holies
To render my flesh
Helpless in the presence of
All that is Him in me and
All that is me in Him

❧

❧

Liberty and Justice for
All
A twisted truth
Lifting up His banner
I rejoice in being a
Patriot of Heaven
Gold and silver have I
None but
He has all the Gold and
Silver
Supplying me with
More than enough
Not as the world gives with
No stability or future
He is God of The
Red, White, and
Blue
His Truth is truly marching on
I will join His troops to the
Sound of a different drum
Which beats loudly in my
Veins
See The Truth
Walk in The Truth
Overcome with The Truth

❧

Barbara Kelly

Shimmers of Light
Coming through a plaid
Curtain
Filters out the harsh
Substance of life
Greater still is the
Filter within
He is called Holy
Remember not the
Former days
Today it behooves you to
Remember only Him
His plan for you identifies
Him in your present and
Your future
He has not nor will not
Withhold from your life all
That He has Promised
These Promises are wrapped in
Shimmering Gold
Bringing substance into
Your hands

Sweet surrender
Goodness and Light
Mercy, Mercy, Mercy
Following me
Not a hair unnumbered
No passing thought not
Heard
Scrupulously looking on
The inside He corrects and
Chastens
With His Perfect Love
Without disdain
I surrender to The
God of my Salvation
The workman is on the
Watchtower
Looking in four
Directions
Foretelling things to come
Do you hear

577

❧

Launching A New Way
A New Path
Comfort comes even
Not knowing the
Next step
When no answer
Seems to come
Alas my heart is sure
The answer is clear
Written so long ago
Acknowledged by The
LORD Of the Harvest as
A feat already
Accomplished by the
God of Plenty
Who holds back nothing
Asked or desired
In agreement with Him and
His Word

❧

578

❧

The goat stands at one
End
The sheep at the other
Swimming deep is the
Blood of the Lamb in
Between
Reckless endeavors and
Righteous ones
We really have no choices
Life comes only through
The Giver of Life
Who has walked
Through all eternity
Toward the cross and
Through the veil
Never surrendering
The purchase paid
Choose life He said.
A goat or a sheep
Which one do You listen to

❧

Barbara Kelly

579

❧

Solutions
Solutions
Man cries
Dumber than the ones
Originally thought
The cry is originated
In a much, much
Lower plane
Where questions have
No solutions
Games are being played
Where no one really wins
Look to the One with all
The answers to all the
Questions
One whose game is not
Known
It doesn't exist
Due to the nature at
Peace with His children
And their trust in Him
Anchor in God
Stretch to new dimensions
Want not
Lo
I am
With you
Always to the end and
Through All Eternity

❧

580

❧

The weather is fine
But the dogs are
Howling at the moon
They know the ever-present
Evil has escalated
The armor the dogs
Wear is made of tin
Not to withstand the
Merciless evil
The moon is wrapped in
Dark clouds
Waiting to drop on the
Unsuspecting
Pull out your Sword and
Shield
Do not fear or
Retreat
Ride, Soldier, Ride
A whisper in the wind
Says the enemy is
Soon defeated
Giving the dogs a bone
Will calm them
Evil is departing

❧

581

&

I have laid the world at
Your feet
Trust Me
The world is Mine to give
Assert your place
According to my plan
I was Born, Lived, Died, and
Arose
So you could command the
Things in Heaven to come
To earth
No longer do My people
Hang on to have victory
Victory lies within
To lead you to the utmost
Redemption with all My
Benefits
I, Who Live, would never
Leave my own without
Prosperity to live as only
Those in My Kingdom can

&

582

&

The snickering crowd
The flesh of your flesh
Seems to desert
But oh
The Glory Of The Lord
Your Father
Remains
Don your robes of
My righteousness
Guard your mind and
Your tongue
My grace in the matters
Overrides the human nature
Do not let satan elude
To the outcome of your
Life
He only lies and does
Not know The Truth
I do
I have leveled the playing
Field

&

Barbara Kelly

583

❧

Soul definition responds
Quickly to benign answers
Living well is not a hoped for
It is The Truth at
work in your life
Nothing is left to chance
If you trust Me
Not only are you in My
Care
There is a detailed plan
Worked out for you to
Follow
Others are watching your
Acceptance of responsibility
In order to promote you
To higher ground
They don't know they are
A part of a Grand Plan
Watch with your eyes only
At the destruction of the
Wicked
I will
I am guiding you to
The Land of Milk and Honey

❧

584

❧

The cantilever is God
Do not pull away
The drop will send you
Into the endless
Possibilities of the
World
I can say these things
Will you ever know
Them by True experience
Don't tear the cloth of
Right standing
From
Your body
Crisis will be averted
While you look into My face
Do as I say and
You know
This will never fail

❧

585

❧

Not withstanding
I say
The crumbling around
You will not overtake
There is a Rock taller
Bigger and more
Rewarding
Go as I told you to
Go not as the world
Says
Lift up your Gifts and
Callings to Me
The very presence of
These Gifts and
Callings
Will guide to the
Everylasting
Plan

❧

586

❧

The length of your days
Is in My remembrance
Collecting dust is the
Money in wrong hands
Monetary value is put to
Things not of value
Would the God of your
Salvation desert you or
Go back on His plan
For you
He has said the Land of
Milk and Honey was just
Over the hill
Just beyond the
Horizon
Contemplate the
Goodness of God as
He shows Himself
Faithful in your behalf
Wonderful Savior
Joy Divine
How to tell of His
Wondrous Glory

587

∽

Above hope is a Glory
Cloud of expectations
Worthless endeavors are
Not a part of My plan
Liaisons are being
Laid out now
To jumpstart your
Destiny
Long for the Higher
Ground
Seek the Master of
The whole Kingdom and
All of Eternity
Listen
Watch and
Wait
The time is short

∽

588

∽

There is a broad leaf
With dewdrops on it
Drink from it
All else is poison to your
Soul
Create a place for
The whole part to
Rest
Search the earth and
All its resources
I say keep focused
On Me and My Glorious
Kingdom
See if I don't pour out
A blessing
Too great to contemplate
Do the immediate thing
Don't look back
My ways are not yours
My ways bring Freedom
Sell all but your soul
And you will find Peace
For you and your family

∽

589

❧

Withholding what is Good
Brings a chatteled existence
Without Freedom
Circle the wagons
Seek only the Leader to
Give you instruction
Sometimes it seems this is
Not enough
Crisis proves the worth of
A circle of friends steeped in
The Blood of The Lamb
Create an opening for
Spirit calling to Spirit
With The God Stamp
There is sweetness in
Cherishing those who
Serve

❧

590

❧

Lift the veil
Clear the smoke from the
Mirrors
The location is a study in
Loveliness
The place is especially
Designed for you
The road is long and smooth
The stranger is coming
To perfect the needs to
Accomplish publication
Do not second-guess
My
Standards and way of
Doing
You both have a job to
Do
Let Me have My way
Little becomes so much
When I have control
This is a smooth transition

591

❧

The breaker has been pulled
The supernatural electricity
Is surging through you
Now
Remove yourself from the
Wicked intentions of
Superficial
Righteousness
Flesh and blood no
Longer hold
You bound
See
Taste
Feel
As I unleash My power in you
Awaken
To a new day
Do not look behind or
To the right or
The left
This is an immediate move
Be ready *now*
The time is *now*

❧

592

❧

Wishing on a star
Brings no results
Seeking
You say
I will find You
Wondering when
Does no good
The effort is
Effortless
You're Always
Present
When I seek

❧

593

❧

A crime has been
Committed
A soft blow
To the soul
Will diminish
All reason
The Lover of your Soul
Says
Seek no revenge
Vengeance is Mine
The Crimson Blood
Provides
Life
Where Life has left
The provider of all that is
Holy
Is your Dwelling Place
Reverence the abilities
He has given you
Deny the grip of those
Following Satan
Remember not the
Former days
A new day has begun
Give it your all
Red is on the
Horizon

❧

594

❧

Swaggering
Staggering
He cannot see
The world
Clearly
The internal compass has
Tilted and he won't
Right it
He has left you without Hope
This is a lie
Kill the one who rules
Him
Seek new surroundings
To buoy your strength
There is a Bigger-Than
Life event coming
to restore you

❧

595

❧

The vocal presentation
Leaves chills running down
My arms
How do you relate all the
Personal knowledge
Without leaning to your
Own understanding
Somewhere in time is a
Platform for the
Whole Truth
Do the unusual things
God cries out to your
Heart to accomplish
Maybe you have not found
The confidence to follow
Through
You can jump without fear of
Falling to a crash
Look to the Unseen Hands to
Hold you

❧

596

❧

A wretched thought
A misunderstanding
Goes on to destroy
Loose the bands
Too tightly tied around
Your heart
Strengthen your vow to
The God of your Salvation
How can you do less when
He alone truly
Understands and
Forgives without judgment
Walk in the faithful Light of
Divine Strength
Times of old were established
In your favor
He was watching and desiring
To pour out His Abundant
Love on you

❧

597

❧

Light the Candle of Peace
See into the darkness
Let Truth prevail
I have asserted My
Place in your heart
Nothing you touch will
Fail
Set on a high hill is
The roster of My
Plan for your life
Sometimes you forget
My Time is not your
Time
But always My Time Is On
Time
Seek the Divine Answer
To the substance of
Life

❧

598

❧

The Listener has listened
The matter has been resolved
In the courts of Heaven
Take heed lest you are
Tempted to arise to the
Occasion of your own
The Overcomer of this world
Has established Heaven and
Earth in your behalf
They are aligned
And nothing man can do
Will undo
What God has established
With Honor and Glory and
Wisdom will bring reproach
To those who wait
To do the right thing
Summon the angels to bring
Forth the Will on God

❧

Barbara Kelly

599

❧

As the flowers bloom in
The desert
So will you blossom in the
Dry places of your life
Your fleeting troubles are
In the hands of the
Mighty God of Israel
Where persecution comes
There is a pathway of
Light to guide you into
The watered and
blossoming place
He says,
Fear not, for I who
Loves you with My kind of
Love
The I Am
Has your back
Covers you with His wings
And delights in giving you
The desires of your
Heart
Sing hosanna to the
King of Kings

❧

600

❧

As you move swiftly
In the LORD
The understanding will come
Winter, spring, summer, fall
Why do you not see
I have a rewarded plan
In which you will find
Satisfaction
Not just business
Crumble the clay that
Cramps your forward
Movement
The most important gift
I have given you is
My Love incorporated
Into you through
Salvation
It is necessary to
Live as I live
Think as I think and
Conduct your life as
I have prescribed
Walk, run, seek, find

❧

601

❧

The willingness to
Be attractive to
Me is
The blessing to Me
That counts
You are offering yourself to
Me, and that is all I need to
Set you into The Place
Come
Let Me have all of you
Let
Me mold you to be
The child of my dreams
Oh
How I want to release
My Knowledge, Wisdom, and
The Secrets of My Heart
So that the ways of you
Will be anointed and
Others will be shaken and
Blessed by your presence
It is My desire
Come walk with Me

❧

602

❧

Assemble the troops
Walk around the bend
See the enemy's stance
Let him know
We win
Truth prevails in a willing
Heart
Complete the circle that
Cannot be broken
Cramping the style of
Almighty God is a venture
In futility
One you will regret
His plan is for success
Not failure
Abundance
Not lack
Seek Him with your whole
Heart

❧

Barbara Kelly

603

Resentment
Is a hard taskmaster
With a relentless stance
His name is revolting
And the destruction in His
Wake is never to end
Unless
You turn from your wicked
Ways to find rest for
Your weary soul
Rest, Peace, Forgiveness
These come at no cost at all
Mulled over with care
Turn 180 degrees from your
Current place to see
How truly wonderful
Life can be
Seek and you will find
Rest, Peace, Forgiveness
From the Author of these

604

A Wise heart knows Me and
Knows Truth from fiction
I am Truth and all else is a lie
As mud slides down a hill
So does destruction in the
Tempter's snare
When rainbows show the
Perfect array of God
We are reminded
of His promise
What a wonderful God
Is He
The cross exists in all
Who have believed
The cross bore the heart of
Love as God is Love
He will not be denied
He will show Himself
Strong in your behalf

605

❧

Where there is even a
Thistle there is release
from tearing

❧

Complete is the work when
God does it

❧

Work, work, work
Won't do these things
Neither fasting or
Long suffering

❧

When God and His angels go
Into the Spirit Realm of
Your life
Not even a flutter of response
From the enemy can
Be heard

❧

Loose yourself from all
Binding situations and
Rise above the enemy
With a Wholeness
From The Throne of
Emmanuel

❧

606

❧

Where there is a vision of
Accuracy
There is Astounding Truth

❧

The very air reeks with the
Perfume of You

❧

Sweep me off my feet

❧

Let me soar to the mountain
Tops while I glimpse of

❧

Things to come

❧

A louder voice than mine

❧

Is in my ear singing

❧

To The Lamb of God

❧

Slain before the foundations of
The world

❧

Barbara Kelly

607

❧

Hope is restored when
Values are kept

❧

Look into the things you

❧

Enjoy the most
I will open the doors
To your future
Listening to My call
Seek not your own
Way

❧

There is a place, and in the
Future, money from
The wicked

❧

They are continuing
To recklessly pile it up

❧

Be not dismayed that
Others prosper

❧

Listen, I will deposit into
Your account

❧

608

❧

The Spirit of God is on you
Right now

❧

The Glory of God is round
About you to bring you
His armament of Peace

❧

Not as the world gives
But

❧

Peace of a type that
Weathers every storm

❧

Hear The Voice of the LORD
Calling you in this wilderness
And sink into Him with

❧

Rest to accomplish His
Purpose in you
Selah

❧

609

❧

Seeker of the soul of man
I seek You

❧

Whither Thou goest, I will go
Whither Thou leadest,
I will follow

❧

Savage situations have
Tried to plunder my life

❧

Triumph says look through
This curtain of despair
To see clearly

❧

That I have overcome the
One who tries to thrust the
Knife into your most
Vulnerable part

❧

Awaken your soul to the
Maker
Lift your heart to Him

❧

He will always honor His
Word

❧

He says we win
By
The Blood of The Lamb
And
Our testimony of Truth

❧

610

❧

A witness to The Truth
Will settle the matters
Before you

❧

A rumble has caused you
To doubt

❧

Stop

❧

Regroup and remember
The Shepherd of your
Life
Always provides what
We have need of

❧

If anyone says otherwise
Rebuke the spirit controlling
The speaker

❧

The Children of God
Rejoice

❧

Barbara Kelly

611

❧

The world is your oyster

❧

The Pearl of Great Price was
Laid there before man to
Weigh by his standards

❧

Not Mine

❧

Your Faith, yes, even this is
Your entry into the great
Good that I have promised
There is no fault found in
Him
Therefore
You have the oyster and the
Pearl without restraint
At your disposal
At your demand
At your call

❧

612

❧

The widowhood of your
Youth no longer holds

❧

You in its grasp

❧

You have been given one
Husband and
His name is Jesus
Today you are in the
Last marriage of the
Time you have on earth
The gold and silver and
All I have is My wedding
Gift
Proclaim to the universe
Behold
The Bridegroom comes

❧

613

✍

Listen
Listen
I am calling your name
The path is before you
Walk, run
Into your destiny
The funds are available
The gifts are in you
The body of believers
Awaits you
Heaven is on alert to
Meet the desires of
Your heart
Come, Dear Ones
I Am

✍

614

✍

Surreptitiously covering the
Reality of God is the
Cloak of heresy and
The words of negative
Confirmation

✍

Levity is a raucous
Clever way to
Beleaguer the mind and
Confuse the outcome

✍

Never in the course of time
Have so many been
Deceived

✍

The Will of The God of
Israel is never
Compromised or
Discouraged

✍

Therefore
I will stand in Victory

✍

Barbara Kelly

615

❧

Dawn has broken
Truth has waged war over
Fact
Simulated conversions are
Uncovered

❧

Christians evoke The Love
To prevail in our being

❧

Living proof is not
Corrupted by situations

❧

The summary of this missive is
We wage war against the
Intruder and
We Win

❧

616

❧

I surrender these expected
Outcomes to You

❧

You, who give unconditionally

❧

Switching rails is a technicality
Of no consequence to the
Conductor with training and
Experience

❧

I've seen the epiphany
I know the confirmation
You give
As You bolster the talents You
Have given

❧

The change will be seamless

❧

617

❧

Sweep the floor clean
Lay the carpet of Grace
Green is its color

❧

Shine your windows and
Mirrors
See without the cloudy
Darkness

❧

Witchery and debauchery
Lay wait

❧

But you have The Power to
Walk on serpents

❧

Listen to the voice on the
Wind
Hold dear and precious
The Words of Jehovah

❧

He has laid down the path for
You to walk where the serpent
Cannot go
This is pleasing to you and in
His sight

❧

618

❧

Where there is pain
Let there be Peace

❧

Surround The Truth with
The Holy Spirit and
Angels to carry it out

❧

Delete the untruth as
We welcome You in
All Your Glory to
Uncloud the darkness
With Light so bright
It cleanses all the
Stagnation of platitudes and
Legalism

❧

There is a switchblade in
The hands of my enemy

❧

I have the Mighty
Righteous, Powerful
Sword of The Spirit
No foe can withstand

❧

Barbara Kelly

619

⋙

Somewhere in the confines of
God's Word is my name

⋙

He knows the essence of my
Existence

⋙

Will the mind come into
Subjection to the Voice of
Righteousness

⋙

Hallowed One in preeminence
Shout with a Shout of Glory
To this earth

⋙

Light of Calvary
Reveal all The Forever
To those of us who believe

⋙

620

⋙

Whither Thou goest
I will go
Whither Thou lodgest
I will lodge

⋙

As I walk by the
Stream in the valley
Pondering Your Goodness
You open my mind and
Spirit to volumes of
Wisdom
How do I compare the
Fullness of Your Presence to
Any other

⋙

Walk with me in this time of
Restless musings
Show me the vast domain of
You
Help me to remember
All this
When darkness is
All around and
There seems to be no Light

⋙

Come quickly, Spirit of Truth

⋙

621

❧

This prickly situation
Resounds with accusations

❧

The prevailing darkness is
Soon overcome by the
Glorious Light

❧

Giving up is not an option

❧

I have said
I will be with you always
Nothing can separate you
From My Love

❧

Do not listen to
Naysayers who come out of
Recent endeavors or those
Who have resurfaced from
The past

❧

My plan is being fulfilled
Even while
The prince of darkness
Has set his sail to plow
Into your ship

❧

Do not cover your eyes in
Despair
Lo, I am with you always
Even to the end of the
World

❧

622

❧

The world is turning
Backward

❧

Where there is Hope
There is Life

❧

Cover your ears
Shut your eyes to
The movement of
Clandestine affairs

❧

Walk circumspectly
Without wavering

❧

I am the Rod and
Staff for You to
Lean on

❧

Come sup with Me
Follow Me

❧

These current
Afflictions are only
Very temporary
Without any lingering
Effect
Sing, dance, laugh
Before Me
I am your Life
Your Future

❧

Barbara Kelly

623

❧

The sword is poised over the
Head of the enemy
Contrary to popular belief
Your answer is not written on
The wind
God sees deep into
Your desires
And is longing to fulfill the
Ones He put there

❧

Create an atmosphere of
Thanksgiving for the bountiful
Measure He is pouring out on
You

❧

He has pledged to give
You the desires of your
Heart

❧

Don't perceive the blessing
By looking at the demonic
Perversion of God's Love
And His Blessing

❧

See the sword as it is
Wielded over the
Witness of doom

❧

624

❧

I hear the rumble of
Horses' hooves

❧

The sound is distant
Ever moving forward
To the rhythm of time
Unfolding

❧

I have not wished upon a
Star
Bur believed in The God of
The Universe

❧

Transformation
Not duplication is the
Source of change

❧

Surrender to the
Splendor

❧

Seize the moment

❧

Keep the flame
Alive

❧

The Bridegroom is
Coming

❧

625

∽

A grain of sand has
Worked into the
Blinded eye

∽

Wiping away the scourge
Leaves scarring that
Won't heal and
Cannot be repaired

∽

Replacement becomes
Necessary
Do not count the cost

∽

Frequently the answer is
Bigger than the problem

∽

Focus on the open door with
Tenacious expectation

∽

Your time has come for
Gentle Hands With a Strong
Grip to
Uphold you
To bring the harvest from the
Seed sown

∽

Secure the doors
And windows of
Your heart to hold only The
Sweet Goodness

∽

626

∽

Leverage is my belief in
The unchangeable
Witness of Father, Son, and
Holy Spirit

∽

Surrendering is my
Pleasure and
Gift to these Three

∽

Honor and Glory and Power
Rise above
Shame, false hope,
And weakness
Do You see The Christ in
Me
Am I a witness to His
Majesty

∽

I bow my knee before The
Almighty God who reigns
In majesty and who is
My Father

∽

Barbara Kelly

627

❧

Hosanna to the One who
Lives in a Cloud Of Glory
Riding a white horse
and wielding
His Mighty Sword
To defeat the one who wants
The throne of my life

❧

Clustered around me are the
Angelic beings looking in all
Directions to stop the plan of
My enemy

❧

I swear my allegiance to the
One Who Loves me
Without restraint

❧

628

❧

The sun will shine
One more day
The tail of the Behemoth is
Swiping at the prophets of the
Kingdom

❧

Mighty men of valor are
Standing taller than He

❧

They are paving the way for
The household of faith to
Succeed with great Pomp And
Glory
With the distinguishing
Traits of The Holy One of
Israel

❧

We are branded by
the Holy One
And cannot fail

❧

The Behemoth is blinded
By The Light

❧

The same Light that is on our
Feet and down our path

❧

629

∽

A listless crowd will
Undermine the most
Brilliant speaker

∽

To do the right and honorable
Is a witness to God's Grace

∽

Swimming in a sea of
Guilt and regrets is
Unproductive

∽

How-to books say you can
Fix any and all things
Without regard for your
Maker

∽

Filter all things through
The Blood of The Lamb
The Light through all
Generations

∽

Forever in His heart
Are the dreams of
The righteous

∽

630

∽

Alive and well are those
Singled out for
Righteousness

∽

God sees the dilemma of
Living in this world and
Not being of it

∽

Look into Him and
Not
At surroundings

∽

The earth is still full of
His Goodness

∽

Little is much when He
Orchestrates the event and
The outcome

∽

Leave the door open for
His good pleasure toward
Those who love Him

∽

Barbara Kelly

631

❦

The riptide has billowed
Over the unjust and the
Just

❦

Welling up in man is an
Unknown voice

❦

Let the games begin

❦

The Fight of Faith is good
The fight is not
Always right or
Good

❦

Seek the Unchanging Voice
To give strength to those
Who hear it

❦

Wrestling with flesh and
Blood leaves tired and lonely
Spirits to invade the
Temple of God

❦

632

❦

The reversal of black and
White
Leaves a mind unsettled and
Confused

❦

There is really no change at all
Just a slight of hand

❦

Disturb the status quo
Walk in The Straight and
Narrow Way

❦

Changing direction only at
The Highest Calling

❦

Weather the storm
Confident in the Unseen
Hand undergirding you
Without failing
Failing is not in His thinking
Toward you

❦

633

❧

Backlash swarming
Like flies
Without further thought to
How we got to this point

❧

Mindless ventures allow no
Promise of brighter days

❧

The crumbling wall of
Blind acceptance will give
Brighter futures to those
Who kindle The Fire
Staying alert to the
Big Event

❧

Close your eyes to the
Windswept plain of
The spirits crying

❧

See only The Hope of Glory

❧

634

❧

To tell of His Marvelous
Greatness
I can only whisper the most
Insignificant telling

❧

Creator
King
Father
Show forth YourMagnificent
Mercy
To this
Your most grateful child

❧

Barbara Kelly

635

❧

Listless musings
Crowd out Good News

❧

Settle the ugly truth
With finality

❧

Leave no openings for
Past recriminations
To develop a stronghold

❧

Withdrawal from
Troublesome witness of
Doom

❧

Life is your inheritance
Blossoming Truth
Brings Joy Unspeakable and
Full of Glory

❧

636

❧

Candy grams from
Heaven impart a frothy
Delicacy beyond compare

❧

A bouquet of roses
Candles to light the
Darkness

❧

Bring Comfort, Joy, and
Holiness

❧

My Love awaits my
Presence in His Kingdom
With great anticipation of
Eternal companionship

❧

I will leave the door open and
The light on
For my Love

❧

637

❧

When winter comes
Look up
Do not look back
The entrance to the
Future
Is The Great Promise of
Fulfilled Destiny

❧

Quickly
Override obstacles to
The Plan

❧

I will wait for You
He says but
Time is shortened
Create a place for
The Glory

❧

638

❧

Lingering shadows of
The darkness must be
Expelled

❧

The Peace that follows
Brings a Joy of huge
Proportions

❧

Seek the way to reestablish
Holy Ground
Where no evil prevails

❧

Walk to the front of the
Line
Secure your place for the
Future
Shut Your ears to the
Mumbling of opposition

❧

The mountain must come
Down
Immediately

❧

❧

My
Tumbleweed
You exercise the freedom of
Spirit when you do My
Bidding

❧

Stony ground cannot
Hold you

❧

You will always flow with
My calling as long as you
Remain untethered

❧

Spring into action as you
Encounter the evil one

❧

Sever all ties that bind
I will teach you by My
Spirit of Truth
Equipping you to
Undertake the task
Ahead
Let it be all Joy

❧

❧

Achievers achieve but
Not for Me

❧

The walking dead seem so
Knowledgeable with no
Blood in their veins

❧

Effectually stumbling into a
Restless grave

❧

Finding little or nothing to
Climb out for

❧

Why do the achievers not
Realize

❧

The Kingdom of
God is at hand
Only those Living Righteous
Bought by The Blood of The
Lamb
Will inherit and receive
The wealth set up for
Them

❧

641

❧

A formidable opponent
Sets up his platform in
Such a way as to overshadow
The Truth

❧

Camaraderie with the
Fallen ones
Brings no satisfaction of
Lasting value
When I look to The Haven of
Peace
My intentions are clear
Living Word is my
Everlasting
Guide
The Penetrating Light
Of Truth shines
Through the opponents
Platform
To reveal the sham

❧

642

❧

Sweet surrender
In the midst of You
Singing songs of old
Around the throne
I'll see soon the
Gossamer and blue
While walking on a
Golden street

❧

I wish, I wish upon a
Star
I see Your face
The touch of Your
Hand
All Is Well In Your
Presence

❧

Barbara Kelly

643

❧

The improbable cause
Is accumulative with all
Attending reckless wandering
No end in sight

❧

Correction of the course
Will produce immediate
Benefits to the
Encumbered lost

❧

A myriad of possibilities
Exist
Look to The Authority of
Your Life
To untangle the If
With a positive approach
To The Possible

❧

That being All Things
In Him

❧

644

❧

Surreptitiously
Diving into the
Unknown
Awaken spirits to
Behold The Faith
You have

❧

No undeserved praise
Should cross your boundaries
Crying to the
Author of feelings and not
The Author of Peace

❧

Criteria for hearing no
Voice but His is to
Cling to and rely only
Upon Him

❧

Crease the fold and
Clean the spots from
Your garments
Awaken to the sound of
His Holy Ones

❧

Sing to The Tune of
Righteousness

❧

Hold up The Banner high
That speaks of His Love

❧

645

❧

We live above the fault line
As we stick together
Live by Faith
Walk down Paths of
Righteousness
Not with the wide road of
The ungodly

❧

Waver not
Live in The Truth of The
Word of God

❧

Facts fly around like
Dust in the wind

❧

Truth shines through
The darkness

❧

The Banner of Love is
My reminder of
Your unfailing
Merciful
Awareness of all that
Concerns me

❧

646

❧

Seeking
You will find
Opening The Door
Gives entrance into
The Holy Gound
I have prepared

❧

Signaling for a right
Turn
Indicates to the bogus
One
You have the guidance
From above where he
Has no influence

❧

Shout to the God of Glory
With a grateful heart
For all that He has done

❧

Sweep the floor clean
Dance to The Tune of
Glory

❧

Barbara Kelly

647

∾

Where there is Peace
There is liberty

∾

Arise and walk
Unhindered by
Withered limbs

∾

Stripes for healing
Were laid upon
His back

∾

Don't let them be for
Nothing in your life

∾

A simple undertaking of
Unabashed belief
Mixed with bold
Faith
Brings victory from
Sickness, disease,
poverty in all areas of
Life

∾

Listen to
The Holy One
Ascribe to His
Wisdom only

∾

648

∾

Hopelessly
Faithfully
Factually
Truthfully
I arise from my bed and walk
I remove these
Blinders and see
I cast off deafness and hear
Nowhere in the
Annals of the time
Is recorded all that You are or
All You have done
Only Heaven reveals these
Astounding truths it sees in
Man
Heaven is not surprised
When the earth groans
When this man
Challenges God then reaps the
Reward of ungodliness
Hope in The Truth never
Changes
Bringing Blessings heaped
Upon Blessings

∾

Turn up the volume
Overturn singular thoughts of
Doom
We are marked for success of
The Divine Kind

∾

649

❧

Swindling the devil
Is my great pleasure
Blindsiding him assures
My victory

❧

Needlessly relenting to him
Stunts the Blesser from
Blessing

❧

Woe to the man who
Cannot envision life
Without sensual pleasures

❧

No one can foresee how
Damaging or long lasting the
Effects of wantonness is

❧

Creating a New Heart gives
God preeminence in
Molding and making a
Plan fulfilled for Him

❧

The side effects of Life In
Christ are rich in every way

❧

Look up and behold
The Untold Goodness of
God

❧

650

❧

My time
Your time
Endless time
Time will be no more
Nighttime has come
Light is on the horizon

❧

Weather the storm
Soon and very soon
The rainbow will
Appear
All creation await
The Light
Stamping out darkness
Forever

❧

Sing to The King of Kings
Put on the bridal gown
His coming is on
The horizon

❧

Barbara Kelly

651

❧

All the prophets
And prophecies
Are true

❧

Your life is recorded and all
That God has planned for you
Is yours

❧

Rendering the enemy
helpless is
Your road to success

❧

The long path to here has
Been but a speck to God
But His heart is tender
Toward you and all that
Has hindered the plan of
God in your life

❧

Sweeter than all the victories
Is your true and faithful
Relationship with Him

❧

Let Freedom Ring
Glory to God And His Grace

❧

652

❧

Leaning toward the right
Shifts the shadow

❧

Do I know the whisper
The shadow makes

❧

Listen to the voice
Speaking Truth

❧

Yield to the passing
Royalty

❧

Bow Your knee to
The God of your
Salvation

❧

There is no time to
Waste

❧

Speak through
Divine Influence

❧

653

❦

Silently I wait
Honoring You with my
Whole being

❦

Your breath on me is sweeter
Than the honeycomb

❦

Body quickened
To The Healing Truth
Washing over me

❦

My understanding is
Enlightened by the
Source of My Salvation

❦

Wisdom regards me as
I beckon Him in

❦

I Have no Truth but
You

❦

654

❦

Sailing over the
Blue, blue sky into
The crystal sea

❦

Leaping through the meadow

❦

Climbing the mountain
With Hind's Feet

❦

I soar with
Wings as Eagles

❦

Living Water refreshes
Manna feeds

❦

My goal is to swing on
A vine
To tell of His
Awesome Grace
Mercy and
Boundless Love

❦

Barbara Kelly

655

❧

Do not censure the
Good I am doing
This is unfruitful
Do not seize the moment
Without hearing My voice

❧

Criticizing the evil done
Does not change it

❧

You must exercise
Compassion for the
One oppressed and
Use my power in you
To annihilate the work of
The enemy

❧

He is the oppressor
Not the one being used

❧

A signal to the Holy Spirit is
Hearing My Word spoken
From your mouth
He will teach you by
Instructing you in
My Wisdom

❧

Show forth the Power I
Have given you to
Overcome the enemy

❧

656

❧

I have given you a gift
A treasure in an earthen
Vessel

❧

I admonish you to use this gift
To administer Peace to the
Anxious and oppressed

❧

Live in My Presence all the
Time
I will take you with Me to
Do My
Work on the earth

❧

Look for Me
You will find Me in some
Unlikely places

❧

Record what I tell you
Proclaim to the masses
My words

❧

My Spirit will guide you
My Wisdom will give you
Discernment and an open
Door
Crush fear
Live freely
Give freely

❧

657

❧

Moroccan nights
With warm salacious
Winds

❧

A purple moon
Stars of sparkling white

❧

Come into The Chamber of
Peace

❧

Allow the Sweet Fragrance
To cancel all other
Remaining smells of
The past

❧

There is a song He sings
To His children

❧

Allowing a knowledge of
Him to awaken the history of
The universe to unfold

❧

His power no foe can
Withstand

❧

Rest In This

❧

658

❧

The Word is written

❧

The Word has been heard
The Word has been read

❧

The end-time of man is
Predicted

❧

Remember Me in this all
Sign no documents
Without My approval

❧

Do not whimper in the
Dark as some who have
Lost their way

❧

Remember the times
Already past
When I took care of
Your every need
Lavishing you with
My precious gifts
Giving you the desires of
Your heart
Let this be your guideline for
The future

❧

Selah

❧

659

❧

Why do you split hairs
When night has already
Come

❧

Wolves are at the door
God is calling you
Away to His Unfailing
Love and Provision

❧

A stalk of wheat is
Waving in the wind
Harvest while you
Can

❧

An unfounded prejudice
Stops the flow of
My Spirit

❧

Will you honor Me
With all you do

❧

This opens the door to
Understanding My means
Even though
Your thoughts will never be
My thoughts or your ways
Mine

❧

My Love is Sufficient in
This time of decision making

❧

660

❧

Mindless meandering over
Uneven ground
Will cause chance to have
Preeminence

❧

Come out of the maze

❧

Willful reluctance to
Follow My voice
Is never productive and
Only brings sleepless nights
With very tiring days

❧

Lift up the hands that
Hang down

❧

Perceive The Goodness of
God that is yours

❧

661

❧

Withstanding
I stand
Not with comely
Features or
A mind of enormous
Potential or
Untold wealth

❧

I stand
Witnessing the demise of
The wicked
With my eyes only

❧

I know The One who
Holds me in the palm of
His hand and who
Shepherds me in The Way
I do not want for
He is with me
Not only now but
Always

❧

You, LORD, have answered
My need and given me
The desires of my heart
Before I have asked

❧

I receive
No questions asked

❧

662

❧

Stay steady
Keep your feet on The Rock
Set your face like a flint

❧

When the waves rock the boat
Stay steady
I am with you

❧

See into the future
With Me, not a
Soothsayer or fortune teller

❧

Lift up the veil that keeps your
Face hidden
Look into My face

❧

Relax

❧

The Bridegroom is Me
I come
Stay steady

❧

No one can take My place
In your life
You have given it to Me
I am The Horn of your
Salvation
Stay Steady

❧

663

❧

The storm has passed

❧

Wake to the dawning of
A new day

❧

Overturn the pot full of
Rain

❧

Relinquishing your hold on
What seems right
But its ways lead to
Destruction

❧

Compare everything to Me
Let Me be your standard and
Guideline
Your measuring stick

❧

Since your time with Me
Before The Foundations of The
World
My watch over you has always
Been complete

❧

See me now as I stand before
You
Waiting to take you into the
Unknown
Be still
I Am

❧

664

❧

Withholding what is mine
Brings sorrow and
Abundant lack

❧

My precious children have
Lost the vision and too
Soon give in to the lies of
The enemy

❧

Stuck in mediocrity is not
Pleasing to you or Me

❧

Simply lay down your assumed
Importance
Look to Me and Live

❧

My Plan is Perfect and Entire
Leaving you Wanting
Nothing

❧

665

❧

I wish you joie de vivre
Viva la différence

❧

Holy unto The King of Kings

❧

A Mighty One in battle
Who sees the triumph
Before the battle began

❧

Wash ashore the lost
Valour will rule
Come into The House of Praise
With the Shout of Victory
Stirring up the downtrodden
With a mighty voice of
Praise

❧

Create an atmosphere of
Peace allowing the
Praise to undulate
Listen to the choir of
Angels reverberating
The Gladness of
God's children

❧

666

❧

If you extrapolate
The future will fall into place

❧

Never underestimate
the lessons
You have already learned

❧

God is watching you with
Perfect Love
While designing your life

❧

Step into the place He has for
You

❧

Sift everything through
The Holy Spirit within

❧

Look and Live

❧

Barbara Kelly

667

❧

The blatant Truth
Has been spoken

❧

You have heard

❧

Now act on it

❧

Boulders have been
Shoved away

❧

A sly hand exposed
Let The Joy overtake
Leave a Glorious trail
Behind

❧

The Awakening is in you
It is a brand new
Day

❧

Just sparkle

❧

668

❧

There are many ways to
Display a fortune

❧

Just know I AM on the
Way to set you in place to
Receive

❧

The investment
You have made
In my kingdom is the way of
Heaven to make
You rich while
I add no sorrow

❧

Look to the world for ideas
But
Use My ways to become
Established in these ideas

❧

Chronological order is the
Groundwork

❧

669

❧

Seek and you will find
Knock and
The door will be opened

❧

Surrender and
Gain complete freedom

❧

Stand in awe of
The Holy One

❧

He will give you the
Desires of your heart

❧

He is your Shepherd
You do not want

❧

Lift up your head
See your Redeemer and
His redemption

❧

Certainty lies only
With the One who knows
You best

❧

670

❧

Cleaver machinations
Fall on deaf ears of
Those united with the
Wisdom of God

❧

If you listen to these
Plots and schemes
Destruction will fall
Hard on your heels

❧

God's eyes of
Wisdom determine
Your outcome

❧

The probability is
That without God's
Purposes being
Implemented soon
The enemy of your
Life will
Rejoice over your
Setback

❧

Look up
Your redemption draweth
Nigh
Rejoice in The One who Loves
You best

❧

Barbara Kelly

671

❧

Voices from the past
Are to be denied
They have taken up
Too much of
Your time
Listening to them revokes
Wisdom

❧

The unleavened bread
Does not rise to its full
Potential

❧

Love the Lover who
Defines Love
Without confusion

❧

The slats are there
To undergird you
When you lie down
When you rise up
The gentle arms of the
Savior will sustain you
When you sit, these
Arms will cradle you
Running will give you a
Companion of great
Strength and
Endurance
Push back the smoke
screen and
See your Lover's Face

❧

672

❧

Wintering in the south
Now coming into the
Place dedicated to The
Unfailing One

❧

I sing with the Heart of
The Ages

❧

Liberation from this
Earthly temple to
Operate in The Spirit of
God

❧

Going where no foe can
Go

❧

My single dedication is
The Kingdom of
Heaven and All Its
Righteousness

❧

673

❧

Listening
I hear
Watching
I see

❧

The elm tree grows
The lotus lives
The fig tree blossoms

❧

When I hear the brook
Bubbling
I Am leads
The green meadow
Is my Peace

❧

To my delight
He leads me

❧

I welcome His
Righteousness

❧

In the valley or on
The mountain

❧

I do not want

❧

674

❧

You are a Fragrant Bouquet of
Lilies and Roses
Blessed with Sweet Dew and
Honey

❧

You welcome me into Your
Mansion not made with
Human hands

❧

Silver and Gold are in
Abundance

❧

Blessings abound in a
Gossamer world

❧

This and more belong to
The Beloved and His
Children

❧

Barbara Kelly

675

❧

Somnolence in the herd
Crying for redemption from
This lost place

❧

Condolences are due
The God of My Salvation

❧

Surefire is the end of
Creation's yearning

❧

Let not the windows of
Your soul remain closed

❧

The prophets have spoken

❧

There is no more to
Do or say

❧

Laid down is the plan
Established before The
Foundations of The World

❧

676

❧

Marauding as a
Prince is the
Enemy's best-laid
Plan

❧

Schiesters abound in the
World all around

❧

Stranger than this is
The Children of God
Listening to and
Following after the
Diabolical plans of
The enemy

❧

Strict attention must
Be paid to the
Armor of God
Which will overshadow
Plans to destroy you

❧

Set yourself free

❧

Situate yourself in
The presence of God
Looking neither right or
Left

❧

677

❧

Leaden feet go nowhere
Untangle the rope
That has you bound

❧

See before you
A table laid most precious

❧

Live your days
Without restraint

❧

Do not allow the bully of
Your life
To speak to you at all

❧

Cremation is the answer to
The dead past

❧

A beautiful crystal glass
Full of wine
Awaits you

❧

Drink of its fullness
Withholding nothing

❧

Hear the lowing in the
Meadow of
His sheep
Beautiful feet you have
That bring
Good news

❧

678

❧

Tremendous effort must go
Forth now to preserve the
Gifts within

❧

No determination of
The enemy will cross the
Blood Line if
You remain diligent

❧

The subtle things must be
Weeded out so as not to
Choke the fullness of
The crop

❧

Crack the window and
Perceive the absolute
Unwavering of
The Goodness of God
Toward you
Who believe

❧

Stretch forth your
Hands and see
Abundance pour into
Them
Asserting the scripture
Saying
Everything your hands
Touch
Prospers

❧

Barbara Kelly

679

❧

When I look into the eyes of
Hope
I see Jesus
Surrender your
Shallow dreams and desires
To The One
Whose dreams are out of
The ages of time
With no limitations

❧

Whether lifting your
Voice in praise or
Speaking His Word over
Your life

❧

He and All of Heaven
Will respond

❧

Let His Dreams cascade
Over you
With Joy

❧

680

❧

Where there is benevolence
I Am there

❧

Pull the resource from
Your spirit to accommodate
The unlovely

❧

Weep no more at the
Place of despair

❧

Walk upright
Looking into The Face
Of The One Who Loves
You Best

❧

He whose Love never
No never
Fails
Sits upon the throne of
The King of Kings
Also reigns from
The throne your
Heart
Let Him sweep over you
Leaving nothing of
Self behind

❧

681

❧

Forever in your Presence
I stand before you
Laying My Scepter of
Righteousness on your
Shoulder
To remind you of the
Nonrefundable gifts
I have given You

❧

Correct the path just
Enough so the shadow
You cast won't interfere
With The Promise
I made you

❧

No longer weep at the
Gate but
Take up your full armor and
Cross over Jordan to your
Land of Milk and Honey

❧

I Am Forever yours

❧

682

❧

The eventide is here
The translucent sky is
Bursting to open and
Display the King of Glory

❧

Willows are weeping
Skylarks are singing

❧

Just the mention of
His name
Causes all creation
To rejoice

❧

Come quickly
God of Ages
With healing
In Your Wings

❧

Barbara Kelly

683

❧

The crumbling facade
Will show The Truth
To all mankind

❧

Truth reveals
What was spoken
Before the foundations of
The world

❧

We will behold
The King of Kings
Without the failing
Sight of
Defeated humanity

❧

Come please
Come

❧

684

❧

Throughout my veins
Flows Truth everlasting
The harmful rays the
Enemy throws
Evaporate before entering
My sphere

❧

The Rejoicing Heralding
From Heaven's Creation
Is from Everlasting to
Everlasting
To declare The Works of
The Lord

❧

Evil Will Not Prevail

❧

685

❧

As I sever all ties
To the past
Moving forward to
The Prize that lies
Ahead

❧

I will seize the
Moment with Power and
Grace
Giving all my thanks
To The God of Creation
Whose Son has set me
Free

❧

He calls me by name and
I listen

❧

686

❧

Sparkling diamonds in
The rough
Waiting to be exposed to
The Light
To transform
From ordinary to
Extraordinary

❧

Who will sing His
Praises
Who will call Him
King of Kings

❧

Truly I call to Deep
With The Deep in me

❧

No telltale signs of
Untruth remain when
Light permeates to the
Uttermost

❧

687

❧

How do the angels
Behave when You give
Your children the benefit of
The doubt
Does Heaven understand the
Magnitude of Your Love for
Me
How do I compare You
To the human understanding

❧

What is my reward for
My behavior
When I don't realize the
Import of things unrepentitent

❧

Never could I repay the
Debt of my sins
My reckless behavior

❧

You Love
You Heal
You Restore
You Redeem
You save from the pit
And Your Love Is
Everlasting

❧

688

❧

The black pool swirls
To expose the
Underbelly of so-called
Sweetness

❧

More than bureaucracy is
Concerned here

❧

It is the intrinsic
Evil of the one who
Looks for the one
To devour

❧

Ours is not to question
Our Father but to
Reconcile with His Word
To listen to His Voice
Without hearing a stranger

689

❦

Step by step
Precept by Precept
Line upon Line
Follow the arrows
That lead down the
Path of Righteousness

❦

That Path Holds All The
Goodness, The Blessing of
God
Which makes you rich and
Adds no sorrow

❦

Diamonds in the rough are
Manifest on this path
Watch for them and
They will enrich your
Life with treasures
Beyond compare

❦

Sweet Breath of Heaven
Pours over you to bring
You Peace
The atonement of extreme
Well-being
The Abundance of God

❦

690

❦

The Rivers of Living Water
Speak more Truth than
Birds of prey

❦

My God reigns in Victory
With the
Conqueror's shield in
My hand to cover my most
Vulnerable parts and
To show my enemies whose
Victorious side I am on

❦

The enemies flee in several
Directions when they see
The Blood on my shield

❦

I dictate the circumstances
By that Blood and my
Testimony of Truth

❦

691

❧

Shrapnel is falling from
The sky

❧

Wars in the heavenlies are
Escalating

❧

To bring us in line with the
Prepared party

❧

No man can predict the time
Of His return but
The signs of war
And rumors of
War tell of the exposure
Soon to take place

❧

692

❧

Lift up the hands that hang
Down
Expose yourself to the
Cause of Victory

❧

Let your voice bring
Sound to the Words of
God

❧

Grasp the horns of
The altar and don't
Let go until you see The
Glory of The LORD in
Your life

❧

Wondrous times are
Just around the corner

❧

Seek and you will find
This is Truth

❧

693

❧

In this present wilderness
My dreams persist

❧

No more am I lost but
Found

❧

Some place is calling
Without restraint

❧

Wells are overflowing with
Springs of Living Water
No more lack in body
Mind or spirit

❧

With You
I am a Thundering
Victorious
Temple of The Living
God

❧

694

❧

Life and the pursuit
of happiness is
Overrated

❧

Where there is Life In Christ
There is Liberty and
The Sosos of
Life
The River of God is flowing
With gale force

❧

Do not fear

❧

The foe is not formidable
He is running fast to
Avoid The Water of Life

❧

Go with the flow
Avoid all forms of strife

❧

Evil Must Flee

❧

695

❧

Deluge of My Spirit
Is available

❧

I love to swamp you
With fire and a Divine
Purpose

❧

Lift Your gaze unto
Heaven and worship Me
I will give you more
Than you have ever
Asked or thought
Faint not
I will be your strength
Body, mind, and spirit
Weep no more
I Am is Your companion
And friend forever

❧

696

❧

The withered hand
Cannot steer
The plow
You have the anointing
To bind and
Loose—not just to
Know this Word
About binding and
Loosening but a
God-given anointing
The ground is waiting
To be tilled
The harvest can be reaped
Search the ground
For rocks that
Would hinder the plow

❧

All is in place for the
Long-awaited
Change God has devised
Start now to give
Him the voice of
Praise and don't quit till the
Withered hand is
Restored to the
Plow, and The Plentiful
Harvest Is
Reaped

697

❧

God requires no
More from you
Than this

❧

I stand at the door and knock

❧

I Am awaits

❧

❧

This present darkness
Shall not prevail

❧

The man of God will sit on
The throne of righteousness

❧

Hearing My voice

❧

Governing parties will
Acquiesce to My plan

❧

Israel will not be
Forgotten

❧

I Will Reign in Victory
As My enemies become
My footstool

❧

Singular attraction to
My completed plan
Is the salvation of this
United States

❧

The mind of the hearer
Will be transformed

❧

698

❧

Will Your Wonder never cease

❧

I give You the essence of me

❧

You give me the essence of You

❧

How does my heart withstand

❧

The Power of This Presence

❧

You fill me to the
Fullest measure
I can only recall Your Word

❧

My eyes look and see only You

❧

The cherishing of You is
My only true Peace

❧

Love and laughter are
Acquainted with You

❧

Your being is resonant
With Your Perfect Love
Toward those who call You
God

❧

699

❧

Scraping the bottom of the
Barrel

❧

Shows me nothing
But the dredge
Of life

❧

Look to the glass half full

❧

Behold the hill where strength
Abounds

❧

See the table set richly

❧

I Behold The Goodness of God
And
Rejoice

❧

700

❧

The ink on the page is still wet
Holy Spirit, blow and cure the
Ink

❧

Set a time in place to
Rectify all wrongs
That have been wrought by

❧

The underhanded sleuth
The broom is sweeping
By itself

❧

Hold up on bitter
Resolutions

❧

The Honor, Goodness, And
Mercy are From
Everlasting to
Everlasting

❧

Go forth in Love
He will protect your
Shares

❧

701

❧

Switching sides is not the
Plan of God

❧

Walk through the valley of
The shadow of death
Do not stay there

❧

Do you welcome the rain

❧

Are You at Peace when the
Breezes blow and birds
Tell of His Presence

❧

Your voice prompts me to
Tell of You and Your Delight in
Your Children

❧

Barbara Kelly

702

Cranial observation says
The dogs have control
Weeping eyes have no vision
Clarity brings a news
Flash
Saying
This is The Day of The Lord
Weep no more, oh daughter of
Zion.
Come and sup with
Me beckons
The Lover of my Soul
Higher up and lower down
All around the town, I
Look and there You are